Watch Out!

Watch Out!

My Autobiography

Jeremy Beadle

CENTURY

Published by Century in 1998

1 3 5 7 9 10 8 6 4 2

Copyright © Jeremy Beadle and Alec Lom 1998

Jeremy Beadle and Alec Lom have asserted their right under the Copyright,
Designs and Patents Act, 1988, to be identified as the authors of this work

First published in the United Kingdom in 1998 by

Century, 20 Vauxhall Bridge Road, London SW1V 2SA

Random House Australia (Pty) Limited
20 Alfred Street, Milsons Point, Sydney,
New South Wales 2061, Australia

Random House New Zealand Limited
18 Poland Road, Glenfield,
Auckland 10, New Zealand

Random House South Africa (Pty) Limited
Endulini, 5a Jubilee Road,
Parktown 2193, South Africa

Random House UK Limited Reg. No. 954009

A CIP catalogue record for this book
is available from the British Library

Papers used by Random House UK Limited are natural, recyclable
products made from wood grown in sustainable forests.
The manufacturing processes conform to the environmental
regulations of the country of origin.

ISBN 0 7126 7920 0

Typeset by MATS, Southend-on-Sea, Essex
Printed and bound in the United Kingdom by
Redwood Books Trowbridge, Wiltshire

My special thanks to
Alec Lom

For Sue, my greatest happiness has been
the laughter I've shared with you.

For Leo and Clare, may you have warm hearts
on cold nights and downhill paths to your desires.

For Cassie and Bonnie, my faith in you is as my love,
boundless.

CONTENTS

PREFACE

This autobiography is an attempt to tell the story from my side. It is intended as a romp of a read. It's not an apology, an excuse or a vindication. It simply answers in honest detail many of the questions people have asked me over the years: 'What was your childhood home like?' 'What was it like being illegitimate?' 'How has your hand affected you?' 'How did you win your first breaks in radio and television?' . . . And so on. I have tried to strike a fine balance between a pacy narrative driven by sharp detail and a story unhindered by needless explanation. This I hope I have achieved.

I have tried to be as truthful as I can. In other words, the stories are as I saw them, or at least, as I have come to see them over the years. But it is only when you sit down to describe your life chronologically that you begin to realise that time contaminates reminiscences with later 'facts' and influences. And we all – consciously and unconsciously – enjoy 'improving the memory'. Why? To make the story better. Upgrade from sword carrier to starring role. Explain past mistakes. Blame others for our own cock-ups.

A good story lasts longer and sells better than a hard-earned fact.

I'm a crazy kinda guy who has lived a chaotic life. Trying to record it in neat consecutive sections has been almost impossible. At many times I have held a number of different jobs, various projects all undertaken simultaneously. I am sure that mistakes have crept into the text and some of the people I have mentioned may well recall the incidents differently from me. And I'm not saying they're wrong. It's just how I recall it.

There are many people who certainly deserve to be mentioned because they are important to me, and we have shared many special and memorable times. To those who feel forgotten, just know that it is only lack of space that has prevented me from including you all. Don't be hurt – you know I love you!

Jeremy Beadle – London, August 1998

1

YOU'VE BEEN BORN!

I was born Jeremy James Anthony Gibson Beadle on 12 April 1948 in a nursing home in Hackney, East London. I don't think the doctors gave me much of a chance to begin with. Even though I survived the first night, I'm told it was still touch and go. I was a breech baby, and a blue baby, and I also had Poland syndrome, a rare genetic disorder which affects one child in every 25,000. It stunts the growth of babies' arms and hands at birth and can also result in webbed fingers. When I was just a few weeks old I was taken ill again, with double pneumonia and enteritis. I had to be christened in an oxygen tent at Whipps Cross Hospital in Leytonstone.

I had many operations on my right hand, and I had to go back to Mount Vernon Hospital every year. Doctors would inspect my hand and take photographs of it. In surgery, they cut down the length of my fingers, which were joined, and I had countless skin grafts and removed amounts of skin from the inside of my thighs, which are also scarred to this day. With all this surgery, I was in and out of hospital for the most of the first two years of my life. There was a girl next to me in hospital called Shirley. She had severe burns and used to cry all the time. Even though I was only about two at the time, I remember her vividly.

Immediately after the War, the family was housed in St. George's Road Leyton, in tiny, cramped accommodation, which was unfit for our large, extended family. So then we were moved to what became, my first home, at Blythe Hill, St Paul's Cray, between Orpington and Sidcup in Kent. It was notoriously rough. I remember seeing people stripping lead off the roofs, and front doors would often go missing. Our house was semi-detached and we lived next door to a family named the Folkes, who we called 'The Folkes At Home'. They had seven children and the family opposite had eleven. Most of our neighbours were very large families who had moved out of London's East End to St Paul's Cray.

Beadle is my mother's maiden name. I was the outcome of an affair my mum Marji had with a married man. When I was a kid, people used to ask me, 'What does your father do?' I would reply quite openly, 'I don't have a father.' Then they'd say, 'Well, is he dead then?' and I would insist, 'No, no. He just doesn't live with us.' There were no such things as single parents then. You were just a 'bastard', and that was that. Some of the locals branded Marji a 'loose woman'. Even on such a rough estate, I think many of the women enjoyed frowning upon her.

I have always regarded the whole business as 'my mum's affair'. I never felt that I had the right to know more about my father. I never even met him. I have seen photographs of him, and read some letters that he sent to my mother, letters which I don't think I was supposed to see. But if I had wanted to know a great deal more about my father during my childhood, Marji would have told me. I have no doubt about that. When I was about nine, I had to go to court. Because I was so disruptive, the social workers were putting pressure on the authorities for me to be removed to some form of boarding school. Marji fought the system tooth and nail, saying I was not a deliquent, nor out of control, and insisting that she was fully capable of giving me everything a child needed. Marji sat me down and told me all about my dad. She explained in simple terms that he was already married.

I know a few more details, but I have never pursued them. He was a journalist on Fleet Street, and somehow that always gave me an edge to believe that I might be able to write myself. Being the product of a single-parent family doesn't make me feel, in this day and age, all *that* abnormal. Today I often visit schools, and I am always very conscious of the need *not* to refer to 'your mums and dads'. In many schools, at least half the kids are from single-parent homes. When people start asking questions like, 'What did you do with your dad in the holidays?' it can cause some children embarrassment as it might make them feel different, or even deprived. But I never felt deprived, and, because I didn't have a father as such, I came to enjoy certain freedoms. Though we had a gang in our street I always ventured further afield to other estates and made friends elsewhere. I suppose I was able to be a bit more of a tearaway than some other kids who had a dad waiting for them at home. In fact, I *did* take more liberties than most.

After I was born, my father made no regular provision for my mum. She had to go to work every day and this used to mean her leaving at about 7.30 in the mornings and not returning until 6.30 at night. When I was a kid, the other children at my school always used to 'go home to tea'. I suppose I was a latchkey kid. My father's promises to support Marji had just evaporated. I read one letter which said, 'I am sorry I haven't sent you any money. Things have been tight.' That would have been sent when I was a few weeks old. When Marji discovered that she was pregnant, I think that more or less signalled the end of their relationship. Today, I don't feel any resentment towards my father at all

3

because I wouldn't know where to target it. I can speak confidently about this subject now because I really never felt deprived. I have never seriously thought about meeting my father. I don't even know if he is still alive. He'd be an old man by now. If he'd wanted to make contact with me, then he could do so. If he arrived on my doorstep out of the blue, I admit I would be fascinated and curious, rather than angry or upset. It would be a bit like meeting a ghost. But what do you say to a ghost? I have often stayed in supposed haunted houses and wondered what I would do if I saw a real ghost – probably I'd blurt out something like, 'Are you happy?' If I did meet my father, I would just say, 'Come on in. Let's have a drink.' There were times when I had to explain that Marji wasn't married, and I always felt sorry for my mum. I felt I was having to somehow defend Marji's situation, but there was nothing to defend, as far as I was concerned.

My mum is very bright and extremely well read. She has also always been a fierce socialist, who believes in fairness and justice. At the end of her long working day, she would busy herself by working to help set up local youth clubs. She felt strongly about the local community and was a staunch defender of the underdog.

One of my earliest memories reaches back to when our neighbourhood was flooded. Many local residents lost their possessions, so I decided to sell all my toys to help the victims of the disaster, whom I'd nicknamed the 'Floodies'. All the children from our area descended on our little garden, where they found all my bits and bobs laid out like a jumble sale. Half my stuff was nicked, but that didn't matter. My gesture contained a sense of justice that Marji approved.

At home, I loved to climb all over the house, swinging from window to window like a monkey. I was always hiding in unusual places. I'd also climb the drainpipe outside, then swing along on to the window ledges. From there, I could leap down and surprise people when they left the house. In the playground at school, I loved climbing up ropes. I was only five but already I was quite mischievous and would love to do things that the others wouldn't. If some area was declared out of bounds, then I would be the first one caught venturing into it. If there was mischief to be had, young Beadle would be there.

Despite the problems with my hand, I was always naturally athletic. I was pretty skilful with a ball, and had that extra element of daring. Whenever I was playing or larking about, I loved danger. I would climb huge trees, then literally start shaking with fear when I realised what I'd done. Opposite us were three whacking great old oak trees in a residential square and I was proud to be the first person in our neighbourhood to climb to the top of all three of them. One day I was showing a boy who lived round the corner the route up, but he lost his footing and fell and was severely injured. I remember him lying on the ground, frothing at the mouth. It was awful. The ambulance came and took him away. I was deeply shocked. Tragically, he became epileptic and died about eighteen months later.

On another occasion, when I was about seven, I walked up into the woods behind our home with my mate Barry Sergeant, who was quite a tough lad who later played rugby for the England youth team. It was snowing hard and we made some toboggans out of old boxes then climbed to the top of a high, rolling hill. I always had to go right to the *very* top, of course, and I'd sit on the front of the toboggan and hurtle down at one hell of a speed, swinging around to avoid hitting a great big tree at the bottom. This afternoon, Barry and I were hurtling down when our toboggan suddenly veered out of control. I shouted, 'Jump!' and I jumped, but Barry, who was terrified, froze in his seat and shot off the toboggan and smashed bang right into the middle of the tree trunk. I vividly remember watching

Barry's face gushing blood into the snow. To this day, he still carries the scar.

My mum worked as a secretary at a firm called Dyn Metal, run by two German brothers named Fritz and Alfred Erle. They were a couple of Jewish émigrés, who escaped from the Nazis by bribing their way out of Germany. They were very thoughtful and kindly disposed towards Marji, appreciating there were times when she would have to be away from work to look after me. In return, it must be said, Marji, who stayed with them for eighteen years, was probably the hardest-working, most efficient secretary they could have hoped to employ. Marji's office was in Victoria Street, just beside Westminster Abbey, and she worked there as a personal assistant. From about the age of six or seven I'd travel up to town with her in the summer holidays. We caught the morning train together, and when we arrived at Victoria Station, I would enjoy exploring the area. Marji was quite happy to let me go roaming about. I can't imagine letting my daughters Cassie and Bonnie wander around London today. Since those early days, I have always felt a passion for London and our country's history. I would head off to see the Changing of the Guard at Buckingham Palace, or to Westminster Abbey.

During term times, I attended Midfield Road Junior School in St Paul's Cray. Many of the parents would take their kids to school, but even though my school was ten minutes' walk from our home, my mum only *ever* took me to school herself on my very first day. She was simply unable to the rest of the time because she had to leave for work long before I set out. On my first day, Marji dropped me off and walked away. I cried – for about three minutes. Then, apparently, I landed myself straight in trouble with the teacher, though I can't remember why . . .

Nevertheless, Marji always made sure I was not left idle. She kept me busy by making me prepare the fire every morning. I used to shake out the coal, rake the ashes, and fetch more coal in. My next task was to go round to the local stores and do the shopping before I went to school, which was a nuisance. I also used to have to buy cigarettes for my nan, Margaret, who lived with us. Margaret was my mother's mother, and was a great character, who came from Liverpool.

Years later, when I made my very first trip to Liverpool, I remember feeling excited as I drove into the city. For some strange reason I felt very much at home there. It was most odd. I couldn't work out why I felt so comfortable and natural being there. It didn't dawn on me until years later that Liverpool was my nan's home. I love the Scouse accent but, funnily enough, while I have vivid *pictures* in my mind's eye of what my grandmother used to look like, I can't remember what she *sounded* like. She wore gold rings on her fingers, on *every* finger to be precise, a touching detail I recall well as she used them to whack me when I was naughty!

My nan (Margaret), who died when I was ten, had been one of the original Tiller Girls, but she was quite a strict lady. She was one of about twelve kids from a large Liverpudlian family. Her father was a purser on the Cunard Lines, which was quite a good job at the time. Margaret had married a hairdresser, disastrously, and they had a son, Ernie, my uncle. She eventually broke up from her husband and moved down to London with Ernie. The family story goes that, one day, when she was very poor and had very little money left, she was sitting on a park bench with Ernie. A man wandered up and sat down next to her, they began chatting and he offered her his sandwiches. Then he arranged for her to find somewhere to stay, and eventually Frederick and Margaret became a couple. They had Eve, my aunt, then, some eight or nine years later, along came my mum, Marji.

Sadly, my grandfather Frederick departed this world as I arrived in it. In 1950, he moved down to St Paul's Cray from the East End, and then he died. I called Margaret 'Nan', or 'Nannie'. And Marji's elder sister was 'Auntie Eve'. She has always been a very dashing, very attractive woman, who must have been quite a flirt in her time. She's lovely.

Nan died when I was ten so my memories of her are somewhat limited. But I do recall that Eve was an outrageous figure – and remains one of my favourite people to this day. She was a very independent lady, who loved life, and always had numerous boyfriends. She eventually married into a middle-class family that was rather wealthy by our standards (I think they had carpets!). Her husband Charles was a handsome, dashing Royal Air Force pilot, who was tragically killed. Eve had three children: Gillian, Vandra and Cherill. Very sadly, Gillian died of gastro-enteritis when she was still a baby.

One sunny afternoon, my mum and I were walking up a local hill near our home trying to fly a kite. Suddenly, this very tall soldier came walking towards us with his knapsack over his shoulder. Quite unexpectedly, he stopped and said, 'Excuse me. Can you please tell me the way to Blythe Hill?' My mum and I replied, 'Yes. It's down there. First right and first left.' 'Thank you!' he replied, setting off. When we returned we learned that the soldier on the hill was Uncle George, Eve's husband-to-be. He turned out to be quite a character. However, their marriage didn't last, although they did stay together for about ten years.

Vandra is four years older than me. We were all raised as brother and sisters at Nan's house. The family love the story of how we staged a party, but had no money, so, as Eve was a naturally gifted seamstress, she started to work. The girls received party frocks and, apparently, I was deeply upset that they all had lovely dresses. So I insisted Eve make one for me. That was my chance to attend the party in a girl's dress. The sight has kept them chuckling to this day.

Anyone who has ever known poverty realises it is relative. You're not aware of your own situation until you place it in the context of other people who are better off than you. Although we didn't have much money in our house, everything was always spick and span. We even had carpets – eventually! Eve kept the plastic cover on our three-piece suite for as long as we possessed it, as she didn't want it to become mucky. Sundays were a big treat because we had chicken. I'd Hoover the house, dust and clean the lounge and bedrooms for pocket money, just a couple of pennies. Marji was fair with me, and if I did anything really neatly, she always gave me something extra.

We would go on holiday to Margate, usually for a week, and stay in a boarding house. My mum and I both loved the seaside, spending the day on the beach or wandering round exploring. Margate had a loud-hailer system for lost children. I heard various little kids receiving name checks when the lifeguards called out to alert their worried parents, so I decided the clever thing to do would be to make myself *deliberately* lost, just to get a name check. My trick worked very well, time and again, until they rumbled me, groaning, 'Oh, no! *Not you again?*' But I still insisted I was lost. Mum and I went to Margate pubs that allowed kids and staged live entertainment. They'd call for volunteers and I remember my mum once went up on stage to conduct the band. The players had obviously been told to deliberately play the notes wrong, which made it even funnier. Since then I have always enjoyed the sight of the public getting up and having a go.

On reflection, my childhood was a very happy one. I was really spoiled at Christmas, when our house turned into an Aladdin's Cave. On Christmas morning, I used to dive down to the end of my bed and find a sackful of toys, thanks to Marji, who used to save up and buy me tons of presents.

Father Christmas had come! What a joy. We were always given oranges and tangerines, the smell of which reminds me of Christmas to this day. One year, I saw my presents and rushed down to sit on the floor, deliriously happy to play with them. I remember Marji sat watching me. I'd been playing with my toys for at least half an hour before Marji asked, 'Have you looked behind you?' I glanced back, but didn't register at first, then did a classic double take! I couldn't believe it – there, on my bed, was a bicycle, a green bicycle. What a surprise. That bike would give me the freedom to go chasing about even further afield. I would disappear from early morning until late at night, cycling everywhere.

I will never forget the Christmas Eve when I was seven. I was sitting on my bed by the window and I saw a flash go past me across the sky. It must have been a comet or a shooting star, but to this day, I firmly believe that the flashing light couldn't have been anything else but Father Christmas. No one else saw this shooting star. Only me. It was obvious: I had seen Father Christmas! I told everyone and they said, 'Yeah, yeah, sure. Of course you have.' For a long time afterwards, my claim became a subject of ridicule. And to this day, *I know what I saw* – it was a flash across the sky.

Kids down our way were always picking on someone. 'Leave them alone,' I'd say. Kids can be rotten sometimes. Where I came from, black people were called 'niggers' and Jews were 'yids'. But Marji told me that was evil, unkind and unfair, and taught me that everybody was a human being. St Paul's Cray was full of guys who had fallen foul of the law and ended up in prison and many hardened criminals lived in our neighbourhood. I knew a few of them. But from Marji I learned fairness and justice. I wasn't tempted to become a swindler or a bank robber myself because it would have somehow been unfair. I believe everybody has a right to their own beliefs. But there are certain things I disagree with intuitively and instinctively. Others, I have intellectually learned, are wrong. But if there's one thing I despise, it's any form of bullying.

One day when I was about nine, I landed myself in a whole bucket full of hot water at school! At the end of the day's lessons, my teacher accidentally left her purse on the desk at the front of the classroom. I was the last one to leave and, as the purse was open, I took a pound note out of it. The following day the teacher announced to the class that she knew someone had taken money from her purse. Eventually I confessed, and had to report to the headmaster's office. I remember standing outside the door of his study quaking with fear. I was so frightened. I decided to run away.

As the school was responsible for me, and because they didn't know where I had gone, they had to call in the police. The whole matter became official and I eventually had to appear before a juvenile court in Bromley, and was placed on probation for three years. I had to report to the Maudsley Hospital, my local authority's centre for psychiatric research, once a week, which took me out of school. It was on Denmark Hill and it meant a long journey – bus, then train, and then a long walk. When I reached the hospital, I would have to sit and talk to the probation officers. On my first visit, they put me in a special room with a woman. I was still only nine years old. We talked for a while and then she said, 'Oh, will you excuse me?' and walked out of the room, leaving her handbag on the table. I sat there and looked around. I saw the bag. I also saw a mirror on the wall and I knew that they were looking at me through the mirror. Don't ask me *how* I knew that because I didn't know anything about two-way mirrors in those days. Somehow I just knew they were looking at me. So I did nothing.

The hospital staff also gave me a series of intelligence tests and reported back that I was a very clever child. I remember the tests were like MENSA puzzles, with various questions involving choosing the odd one out. I loved them. I remember one featured a thick book full of pictures and I had to say what was wrong with them.

It wasn't only at school that I liked to play pranks and mess around. One of the favourite games I liked playing with all my friends on my estate was Knock Down Ginger. It involves a fair bit of running around, as you knock on someone's door, then sprint off and hide. The poor victim opened the door and would find no one outside. Then, I would return to the same door and knock on it again. Once again, the occupant would be puzzled why nobody was on their doorstep. For me, the game was all about how often I could dare to go back to the same door. I knew, sooner or later, that the person living there would twig what was going on. They would stand right behind their door waiting, so that as soon as you knocked on it, they would open it – and catch you. But I was wise to that. I knew that the third time I knocked, the occupant would be ready to trap me, so, I fetched a line of string, tied it to the door knocker, and hid in the bushes. As I pulled the string, the door would rattle and they would snatch open the door immediately. And, again, no one would be there!

But I had one final door-knocker trick, the most daring one of all. There were small ledges or parapets above some of the front doors. When the occupant was really fuming, I would climb up on to the parapet, then, I'd rattle the door with a stick and tuck myself back up. As soon as they heard the noise again, the occupant would rush out, see no one and go back indoors. So I'd do it again.

Many of the mod cons that kids today take for granted were never a feature of my childhood home. We didn't have a telephone until I was about sixteen. Nor did we own a television. I'd visit Mrs Irvine next door, along with other kids, to watch the first television in our street. It was black and white, obviously, and had a tiny screen, the size of a Walkman. I loved watching *Andy Pandy* and *The Woodentops*.

My mum was a liberal, free-thinking person, who gave me a great deal of freedom and trusted me to do all sorts of things from an early age. She gave me responsibility. I suppose not having a dominant father figure around must have had some kind of effect on me as I grew up. That's what some people claimed. It upset Marji because she deliberately allowed me freedom. When people said things like, 'That boy needs a good box round the ears!' Marji would fiercely defend her corner. I'm very much like my mum, and expect to find fundamental qualities, the basic courtesies, in other people. I also see my own personality in my daughter Bonnie, who's now ten. I am, as a rule, very tolerant towards her but when she strays seriously out of order, then I lay down the law. I say, 'Don't do that!' Then, when it continues, I say, 'Right! Now I've asked you not to do it, so please don't!' And when *that* fails, then I say, 'Fine! The next time you do that, you're going to regret it. You know I will do it and you won't like it . . .' And that's normally enough. If my children really lose control, then I am the bottom line. By contrast, there was no absolute real bottom line in my own childhood. Though my mum married later on, Harry wasn't my proper father. I suppose a number of people have attributed what I am today to the psychological impact of my not having a father early on, like some of our neighbours claimed all those years ago. But I have *always* hated being told what to do. When I am called upon to be civil and asked to do something, I can be most obliging, but that always relies on respect. Or the lack of it. I never believe that, just because someone wears a uniform or holds a particular title, they have authority over

13

another person. As a boy, I was fairly independent and not having a father around did probably make it easier for me to challenge authority. But I have always been aware of not wanting to upset people. Mind you, I didn't mind *offending* people, because often you're only pricking their own self-esteem or their prudishness.

The real contradiction is this: I am very curious about the private lives of famous people. I feel personal details provide a great insight into their character, decision-making and development. But although such matters fascinate me, I am also calculatedly uninterested in my own father. I know of endless stories about people who were adopted or given away as children, who yearn to go back and meet their real mother or father. Not me. Perhaps they feel that way because a huge chunk of emotion was missing from their lives. But I had an abundance of emotion, and never lacked affection or love or protection.

I find it difficult to convince people that, in my heart, I genuinely feel I would be treading on my mum's ghosts if I were to start investigating my past. I'd be doing it for purely selfish reasons, just because I was curious. 'If you want to make contact with your father, we can arrange it,' Marji told me when I was really young. I replied, 'No, there's no need.' Now, if I were to seek out my real father, it would feel as if I was 'invading' him, because I haven't been invited. My father, if he is still alive, would probably think, 'Why hasn't Jeremy sought me out before?'

The truthful answer is that I respect that he has a life of his own and I can see his point of view. My father was married. He had children, two kids of his own, I think. He had an affair with somebody. She became pregnant. What do you do? It is a nightmare confronted by many people. For me to suddenly turn up on his doorstep would be an invasion of his life, and it would, I suspect, also upset his wife and his children. Would I want to do that, just so that

I could meet and link up with the person who shared my creation? What would we talk about? We have absolutely nothing to share with each other. The only thing that my father could really talk openly to me about is the affair that he had with my mother. And that is their business.

The only thing that my father would have been sure to know and recognise over the years is the name of his son, the name Jeremy Beadle. It's a name that's been in quite a few newspaper articles, and as my dad was a journalist, he would presumably read magazines and newspapers. He would know, too, that my mum is Marji. He would not be blind to those facts.

When I was very young and discovered the letters between my mother and father, I read them all, although I knew I wasn't supposed to. The letters became shorter and shorter as time went by and were always full of apologies for not sending Marji money. I don't even know how old my father was when he had his affair with my mother. It would be very easy for me to find out, I guess, but if he was thirty-five back when I was born, he'd be eighty-five now, if he were still alive. As far as me and my father are concerned, we are talking a lifetime apart now. I have always admired my mum for the way that she coped with a very naughty child, surviving on very little money and without support of any kind from my father. I guess I should feel quite curious to meet my father.

I once gave an interview to a newspaper journalist called Ivan Waterman. We talked about family matters and then he went away and wrote an article under the banner head-line: 'MY DAD DUMPED ME AT BIRTH'. My mum was understandably mortified. It was a typical piece of trashy press so I was able to shrug it off, but it was different for my mum. I was upset for her.

If my father is alive and reading this book today, I think my message to him would be this: 'Father, I hope your life

15

has been as rich and as full as mine.' There's absolutely nothing missing in my present life, or my past history, that his presence could have improved. My father can be pleased to know that, if he felt guilty at any time, he should now feel relieved that I feel I didn't miss out on a thing. Marji made up for everything.

Other people who read this will never have known their father and gone through exactly the same dilemma. They may be surprised by my comments, but I also hope that what I have said may help in some small way. Many people have an almost genetic need to meet their father. And I can understand that and sympathise. But, equally, please do not think me a cold fish if I say I'm not interested.

Having never met my own father in his lifetime, I would not wish to commemorate his death by attending his funeral. If his widow asked me then I probably would do so for her sake. I would imagine that my father had obviously talked to her so she therefore wanted the secret to come out to give her a release in some way.

By now, I imagine my father must be dead. But if he is still alive . . . I wish you well.

2

SCHOOL FOR A SCOUNDREL

When I failed my eleven plus, my exam result mystified my probation officers and my school. They couldn't work out why I had done so badly. All their tests had shown that I was above average intelligence, but I suppose I was always in trouble, and I didn't concentrate on my work. It saddened me because it meant I had to split up from my gang of school friends. Some of them went on to technical schools, others to the local grammar school. Midfield Secondary Modern School was located only about three hundred yards from our home. It would have been ideal, even though it was a very rough school, but they refused to take me because I was considered a disruptive influence. So, at the age of eleven, I ended up moving to Orpington Secondary Modern, which involved a really long journey to school every morning. I had to catch the bus at twenty to eight, which meant a journey of about forty minutes, involving a change of buses. The second bus would take me to the bottom of the road where my new school was, but I still had a further half-mile walk up a steep hill. So every day began with a long and arduous journey, but I looked forward to it though, because I met so many different people from all the various schools in our area. The trip was my chance to strike up new friendships – a breath of fresh air, because at my previous school, Midfield Road Junior School, I had had a bit of a rough time. Mr Taylor, the headmaster, had been pretty tough. And Mr Brock, whom we nicknamed 'The Bullying Baldie', used to whack us. He hated me and I hated him. Bald, with red hair down the side of his head and high cheekbones, he looked very fierce. He used to fly off the handle over any trivial matter and Beadle was guaranteed to work him up into a lather.

I have kept quite a few of my old school reports from that time. In one, from 1958–9, when I was about ten or eleven, Mr Brock said: 'Jeremy has, I think, had a good year. Generally, he has settled down to the job in hand. I think he lacks some self-confidence when tackling written exercises for he asks questions to which I have found he knows the answers.' He added though: 'On the whole, Jeremy is a vastly improved boy.'

The truth was, of course, that I would *intentionally* ask heaps of questions, just to interrupt the lessons because they were so boring. Asking questions was always much more fun. Mr Brock would rattle on with the answer but nobody was remotely interested in what he had to say. By asking so many questions, I would ensure that lessons passed by more quickly.

I remember a big row in class. I said that Charing Cross was north of the River Thames in London and he insisted it was on the south side. I replied, 'No, it's not. It's *north* of the river!' I knew I was right because of the summer holidays I had spent exploring London, so I considered my position, then said to Brock, 'You're wrong!' He came over to me and whacked me round the head three times. 'Don't you argue with me!' he said, as he hit me on the back of the head with his hand again. He also used to cane me on my left hand, and hit me with rulers, and throw blackboard rubbers and chalk at me.

18

I used to have my revenge by soaking his chalk in water so it couldn't write on the board. The blackboard itself was on a roller system, which provided plenty of fun too. I would write Brock special messages. At the top of our board, he always wrote the date and I would change it while he was out of the room. Then I used to jam things round its back, so that Brock was unable to roll it. I also used to load it with confetti, a whole box at a time. Mr Brock would write on one section of the board until it was full, then he would grab the roll and, with a big jerk, rip it down. He should have been at a white wedding!

At Orpington County Secondary School, I received what is probably the worst report in the history of school education. When I was in Class 5C, I had a sports master named Jones, who used to fancy himself at football and push everybody around. I once had the great pleasure of deliberately tripping him up on the football field, much to everyone's delight. I had to run like crazy to escape because he really lost his rag. He got his own back when he said nasty things about me in my report dated February 1964. Then the headmaster Willingham chipped in the following:

I am very disquieted at Jeremy's extremely poor result, which is entirely due to a foolish attitude to work that bodes ill for the future. Jeremy has gifts but lacks the self-discipline and humility to use them.'

My 'foolish attitude' may have been the result of the school's lack of ability to make education fun. I'd always loved learning. But they took the view that I was failing the education system – whereas, looking back now, I might equally maintain that their system failed *me*, especially as no student was more eager to learn about life than me.

I always hated bullies. One particular pupil was very threatening, so I decided to teach him a lesson. He always

19

Watch Out!

KENT EDUCATION COMMITTEE

CHISLEHURST & SIDCUP AND ORPINGTON DIVISION

ORPINGTON COUNTY SECONDARY BOYS' SCHOOL

Report  Sheet

Name...... *Jeremy Beadle* ......　½ Year ending *Feb. 1964* ......

Form ...... (5X) 5S. 5 ......　House. *Livingstone* ......

Subjects	Standard of work	Effort made	Subjects	Standard of work	Effort made
Scripture　...　...	—	—	Arithmetic ...　...		
English Composition	2	B	Algebra　...　... Geometry　...　...	5	C.
Literature　...　...	—	—	General Science　...	4	c.
History　...　...	5	C.	~~Gardening~~ TECHNICAL DRAWING	5	C
Geography ...　...	—	—	Metalwork ...　...	5	B
French　...　...	5	B	Woodwork ...　...	—	—
~~Art~~ BIOLOGY　...	5	B-	Physical Education	3	B+

NOTES:

1.　Pupils of each year are put into Forms according to their work and ability.　The whole range of Forms for a pupil's year is given in order, and his actual Form is ringed.

2.　Standard of work means in comparison with other boys in *the pupil's own Form* and is in five grades—from 1 (very good) down to 5 (weak).

3.　Effort made is assessed in three grades, A, B, C.　A means that a pupil has worked hard and to the best of his ability; B that he has shown satisfactory interest in the subject; C that he has been disinterested and inattentive.

FORM TEACHER'S REMARKS.

A very poor report — the result of very little if any work.

....

Form Master or ~~Mistress~~.

I am very disquieted at his extremely poor result, which is entirely due to a foolish attitude to work.

S.E. Willingham

Headmaster.

which bodes ill for the future. Jeremy has ... but lacks the self-discipline

The next term begins on........................

and humility to see them.

20

used to park his bike at the front of the school, a VIP parking slot which was considered to be somewhat exclusive. One day, a delivery lorry drew up and parked right outside the school gates, near a lamp-post close to the fence where this guy had parked his bicycle. He only used to lock his front wheel so, during the break, I went down and removed the wheel. Then, I picked up the frame without the front wheel, and climbed up on the bonnet of the lorry, hauling the bike with me. Next, I clambered on to the roof, carrying the bike, which I hooked over the very top of the lamp-post so that the middle of its frame slotted over the light. Then, I carefully lowered the bike to the ground. After school, the guy came back to find just his single bicycle wheel chained to the fence and the rest of his bike hooked over the lamp-post. By now, the lorry was long gone, so of course, he couldn't work it out!

Being caned was a regular occurrence. If anything ever went wrong at school, or if there was ever any outbreak of chaos, pandemonium or disruption of any kind, I was always in the firing line. Another teacher, Mr Wrin, was a wonderful, precise man who taught technical drawing and mathematics, which, unfortunately, were two of my worst subjects. That was really disappointing because I liked him. This entertaining and interesting man could tell a good story, and he used to impress us by explaining how he could dismantle a car engine wearing white gloves without dirtying them with a single mark. When Mr Wrin punished me, he regarded it as a special occasion for the entire class to savour. Me being whacked marked 'an event'. He owned a selection of slippers of different sizes. They were really tennis plimsolls and he would select a size according to your offence. He would chalk a swastika on to the sole of the slipper (*not* an indication of his political sympathies), then he'd tell you to bend over. Again, depending on the gravity of the offence, he would take either one, two, or three steps

21

backwards, then he would come running and whack you on the backside. It always really hurt but if the chalk imprint of the swastika was not imprinted clearly on your trousers then he would go through the whacking routine all over again.

I'm afraid I wasn't very good at art either. In fact, I was appalling. I must have 'lost concentration' at least once or twice during art classes. My art master, Mr Jenkinson, was a tiny man but he used terror tactics. If I had done something wrong, he made me stand up, there and then. 'Right! You! End of class!' And I would have to wait through the class knowing that I would be whacked at the end of it. And it really hurt. He kept a cupboard on the wall of the art room which contained four canes, and to each one he gave a name. I remember one was called Matilda and another Lily. They ranged from very thin and swishy, to rather thick and brutal, and again he chose the cane size according to the offence committed.

I frequently received canings with blackboard rulers, canes and slippers, either on the hand or on the backside. For more serious offences, I had to stand outside the head-master's door, which was awful because the anticipation was far worse and more terrifying than the punishment. I was probably caned once a fortnight, and general whack-ings were even more frequent.

At around this time, I developed a fascination with hypnotism. I found a book on how to hypnotise people and used it to put my friends into a trance. There is no great mystery or mystique about hypnotism. It's just a state of sleep that people can be led into in differing degrees. I used to hypnotise people by sitting them down in a chair and asking them to relax. 'I want you to imagine it's a warm, sunny day and that the sun is beating down on you,' I'd tell them. Then I would start counting, from ten back down to one. 'Each time I say a number, you're going to fall into a deeper, calmer, more relaxed sleep. You are really enjoying it.' By the time I reached the number one, they would be genuinely hypnotised. I also tried regression, which takes the subject back to a time when they were younger to learn what they were doing at the time. I also made them do different tricks under hypnosis, inducing them to raise their arm in the air and then to hold it there, or to stick their fingers up their noses, or run around like a duck. I would also make them go rigid, like a board, so that I could sit on them, putting their head on one chair, their feet on another chair, then inviting others to come and sit on them too. The person under hypnosis could not move.

Concentrating hard during hypnosis was really important, as I discovered on one particular occasion. When I was about fourteen or fifteen, I hypnotised a girl called Karen and took her back to the age of nine. When I thought we had finished, I woke her up again. But I hadn't properly brought her back to the present day and she wandered around looking like a terrified little girl. She didn't know where she was and could not identify anyone else. Everybody was thrown into an absolute panic.

In times of crisis, I have always been very cool and logical. I can halt panic very easily. I had the problem of putting her back to sleep because she was still a nine-year-old, so I calmed her down, sat her in a chair and brought her back to the present day. All I had to do was treat her like a nine-year-old and offer her reassurance. 'There's nothing to worry about. Your friends are here. We're just playing a game.' She was wide-eyed like a frightened rabbit, but then I made her close her eyes again, calmly and gently comforting her, and talked her back to the present day.

Apart from a couple of old school reports, I haven't kept anything from my school days, not even a class photo. But I do remember that the only time I ever had any encouragement from any headmaster was during one summer holiday.

For our vacation homework we had to read a book and visit a place and write a piece on each. I visited the House of Commons, and wrote up its history, sticking pictures of it in a book. The book I read was, at my mum's suggestion, *The Diary of Anne Frank*. I was completely moved and impressed, and took a great deal of care and time producing my essay on it.

When I received it back after marking, I found that, at the bottom of the page, the headmaster had ticked it and added the word 'Good'. Strangely enough, I have always remembered that brief moment because it marked just about the only time I ever had any encouragement or real praise from him. Three years ago, I was asked to open the Anne Frank exhibition in London, a travelling educational exhibition which was beautifully arranged and very moving. I felt very flattered to have been asked as I'm not Jewish, although I have many Jewish friends and do a fair amount of work for Jewish charities, and my mum's future husband Harry was also Jewish. In being asked to open this exhibition, I was really invited as a celebrity. In my speech I told them about Anne Frank and the essay I had written at school years earlier. I told the audience it was the only thing I'd ever kept from my school days. Then, I added, 'If you don't believe me, here it is!' and I pulled out this essay. Everyone was very touched by the fact that I had something personal to say and, in the end, they decided to include my old school essay in the works on display at the exhibition! I was both surprised and honoured.

When I was about sixteen, I used to have great fun staging shows in our neighbourhood. One friend of mine, Geoff Westley, was a pianist and flautist, and together we used to write comedy sketches. There was a ballet school nearby and I'd invite the girls to come in and dance for us as well. With their help, we put on quite a few shows for charity.

While I was still at school, my mother was very active at our youth club on the local estate. Previously, there had been no facilities whatever for the kids. Marji was part of the committee that established the club, which I am proud to say is still running today. One of my early and rather dubious moments of stage stardom came when I made my debut as a pantomime dame at the youth club. Naturally, I rose to the occasion, making my entrances with a flying head roll across the stage from the wings – in full drag remember! During one of the dame scenes, when I had to wear a ludicrous swimming costume, I made sure that my nether regions were well stuffed with socks. It brought the house down. I caused absolute chaos and a near riot on another occasion when there was 'a slush item' which involved food being hurled at the audience during cooking scenes. I thought it was hysterical. Every night the producer Mrs Westwood warned me I must behave. But I carried on with the fun, and the public loved it.

Letting my hair down at the youth club further encouraged my sense of rebelliousness. I already had a widespread reputation and a long history of mischief. I had been involved in CND and Oxfam, which my school didn't approve of, but CND appealed to me because my mum had always been a fierce socialist, and she allowed me to attend the meetings, even though I was still at school, because she believed they were part of my general education. It was a great joy to have the opportunity to meet so many intelligent, interesting people. I would often be the youngest person there, and I'd listen intently as all these intellectuals sat round debating the issues. I felt very comfortable in their company and I was fascinated to hear people speaking so passionately about their beliefs.

To suddenly find myself in a group of vibrant, passionate people was a thrill. I vividly remember going back to school and thinking everybody was rather dull by comparison.

Even though I read tons of books, I was always bored at school. I am sometimes amazed at the number of books I would consume. I wasn't exactly a bookworm, because I was too busy charging about doing other things, but I read a great deal. Strangely enough, although the resemblance may not be immediately apparent to you, I always took comfort from Winston Churchill, who was also considered a dunce at school. When asked why, he replied, 'Because they never asked me anything I knew.' Likewise, they never asked *me* anything I knew. I had a terrific general knowledge but somehow I felt that my teachers never made school exciting or interesting. School was just a factory, where you sat on an assembly line and came out at the end of your shift fitting the expected specification.

I took part in CND demonstrations and twice went on the famous Aldermaston marches. On both occasions, I was arrested and fined for disturbing the peace. They were sit-down demonstrations and we were all carted off by the police, and I was summarily taken into a specially convened magistrates' court and fined. But the marches were terrific fun. They were three-day events, and you had to spend two nights out. They were great adventures for a fifteen-year-old.

To raise money for Oxfam, I once went on a three-day fast in Orpington High Street and throughout my fast, I collected money for the charity. My headmaster tried to stop me, calling me in and saying, 'Beadle, this is disgraceful! You shouldn't make a public display like this.' He gave me a real dressing down, but he couldn't stop me doing it – and he didn't.

Because of my long history of creating mischief and mayhem, my studies suffered and we were approaching our mock O levels. I had done virtually no work and my results were, in contemporary terms, minimalist, to put it mildly. Those poor exam results, my endless rows with the school staff, my frequent truancy, my lack of application – all came to a climax one day. The headmaster pulled me into his study. 'Look, you are obviously not doing any work, so there seems no point in keeping you here', he said. 'I have telephoned your mother, and I have decided that I wish you to leave the school. I want you to go straight back to your classroom, pick up your bags, and leave. Now.'

I was shocked. When I had been summoned by the headmaster, I thought I was just going to be given a dressing down or a caning. But I had been told to leave immediately. It was sudden and dramatic.

I remember slowly walking back to my classroom. Everybody, all my classmates, were wondering what had happened in the headmaster's study. I just gathered my books and packed my bag. Everyone started whispering questions. I just replied, 'I've been expelled. I'm leaving. That's it!'

My friends were all open-mouthed. Mr Jenkinson, the geography teacher (no relation to Mr Jenkinson the art teacher), saw me out as I made for the door. I walked out of the classroom, then passed through the school gates. As I did so I felt an immense sense of relief. I was also flushed with a wave of excitement. I remember thinking, 'Thank God it's finished and done with.' I knew how prisoners felt when they were released from jail. In an oddly similar way, I too felt that I had 'served my time' at the school. I knew that my punishment was over. In an instant, I realised that my whole life was ahead of me now. I could make of it whatever I wanted. I could be anything I wanted.

I meandered about a hundred yards down the road, then suddenly stopped in my tracks and thought to myself, 'What the hell am I going to do!?' I arrived home to discover that my mum had also come home early. She said, 'You've brought this all upon yourself. You deserved it.' My leaving school this way was a bitter disappointment to Marji, who

27

always believed in me and was convinced that I had great talents. She was always so very proud of me, despite my not having given her that much to be proud of. I felt I had let her down but I didn't think I had let myself down. Throughout my troubles at school, I always maintained this strong inner belief that I genuinely had something major to offer the world.

My mum turned to me and asked, 'So, what are you going to do now then?' I sighed a long sigh, then replied, 'Well, I guess I'll just have to find myself a job.' And with that, I put on my coat without another word and went out to buy a copy of the *Evening News*.

Despite my mother's feelings of sadness and disappointment, I was burning inside. Burning bright with a sense of excitement. I knew exactly what I was doing. I was going outside to meet the world.

3

GROW UP?
WHY ON EARTH SHOULD I?

The morning after I was expelled, I remember going down to make myself a cup of tea, thinking, 'Great! Now I don't have to go to school any more.' I thought of all those poor sods in my class who were still beavering away at their lessons and I heaved a sigh of relief. I was free at last. But as it also slowly dawned on me that now I had a whole day to fill, I started to feel rather restless. I do recall feeling excited at the prospect of actually being 'adult'. I firmly believed that, at the age of fifteen, once you started work, you were an adult. And for a person who has never grown up, that was a strident ambition! I went out to look through the daily newspapers to search for work. My mum warned me that, in her view, the only work around was in factories. I told her, 'Right, I'm off! I'm going into town to read the *Evening Standard.*' In the paper that day, I saw a vacancy for an insurance clerk and I rang them up and convinced them to give me an interview. I lied through my teeth in order to get the job, stressing how I felt a career in insurance offered a wonderful future for a young man like myself. I reported for work the following Monday morning at an office in London in Great Smith Street, just round the corner from

Westminster Abbey, an area I already knew very well.

It was a tiny office with a small staff of four young women, ruled by a huge eagle-like man, who was very proper and wore great big pebble glasses. He was an awful boss because he demanded that everything be done in a very exact and precise manner. I used to travel up and down to work thinking, 'There *has* to be more to life than this.' To brighten up my day and cope with the boredom of mind-numbing tasks, I used to 'mix and match' the files. If I thought an application form was a bit dull, I would simply improve it. For instance, I would change the profession from 'salesman' to 'deep-sea diver' on the form so that, by the time I'd finished 'sorting' the filing, all their clients led much more interesting lives. So that was my first job at sixteen, and my *first* sacking!

After that, I was sent along to meet one of my mum's friends who was the head of exhibitions for what was then Iliffe Press (which later became IPC Magazines), based in Stamford Street, just across the River Thames. I was employed as a messenger in the post-room, sorting out the mail and delivering it to the different trade magazines housed in the building – *Amateur Photographer, Motorcycle News, Nursing Mirror, Cage and Aviary Birds*. It was a big building, employing many young people ambitious to break into publishing. I had heaps of fun there. Best of all, it was a really sociable place to work. I used to organise coach trips with all the messengers, and we used to go down to Southend where I staged parties. I would hire the coach, fix drinks for the journey, collect the money, and produce the whole event, gathering everybody together.

I remember one trip to Southend when we asked the driver to pull up right beside the sea. I leaped out of the coach and ran straight into the sea with all my clothes on, just for a lark. It was a bright, sunny day and this seemed like a joke at the time. I came out absolutely soaked through, and ended up regretting it for some time as my clothes went clammy and stuck to me . . . We visited the big Southend funfair and, still dripping in my wet clothes, I went on the Rotor, one of those giant drums that spins you violently as you stick to the sides by centrifugal force. I discovered that, if you were very daring, you could shuffle down to the floor, which had by then fallen away because you were safely stuck to the sides. Then you could lean forward, and touch the centre. Great fun! Unfortunately, I hadn't allowed for the fact that salt water had now seeped right through all my clothes and they had started to shrink. When the giant drum started spinning, the seat of my pants started ripping. And I don't just mean a little tear – they ripped right across the seam from side to side and I had to walk around with an enormous gaping hole in my trousers. What a sight! I spent the whole day with my arse hanging out, literally. Come to think of it, I seem to have spent my whole *life* with my arse hanging out!

At the time, I was earning about eight pounds a week, but after a year I was promoted to selling advertising space on the trade magazine *Electrical Review*. Because I have never been shy, and also because people recognised me as a talker, it was automatically assumed by my bosses that I was a natural salesman. Wrong! The truth is that I am *not* a salesman at all. I am an enthusiast, and there is a big difference between an enthusiast and a salesman. The trouble I had being a salesman was, fundamentally, that I always ended up telling the truth. I could whip people up into a frenzy but then I'd go and spoil it all by adding, 'Ah well, but I really should tell you so-and-so . . .'

Nevertheless, I felt I was reasonably successful. Selling on the phone was just play-acting for me. I could be convincing on the telephone, mainly because people never knew I was only sixteen. And I never ever used to tell anybody my exact age until I was much, much older. Being on the telephone enabled me to be a master of disguise, and I worked out that I could make myself sound much older and more important.

Anybody who has ever been in advertising will tell you that you always end up with holes, which as a final resort you fill with 'house' adverts for other magazines in the company, though this means that the magazine is earning no revenue from them. So, I discovered that I needed to offer those spaces at any price. It didn't matter what the advert was for, because it was all income. I used to invent wild stories to clinch those last-minute adverts, ringing up a client and saying that my bonus depended on filling *one last space*. So I would appeal to them to help me out, and sell the advert at a rock-bottom price.

I was always stealing adverts from the other salesmen. If I saw an advert in another in-house title that I felt would suit my magazine really well, I would ring the client who had booked it and say that unfortunately the other rival magazine had had to drop the advert but I could offer them a special deal in my own magazine instead. My trickery didn't exactly please my colleagues when they found out, but it did keep my sales figures pretty high and I soon acquired a reputation for filling those spaces.

Over the years, I have been a major supporter of distillers up and down the country, as my friends will confirm, and it was during my stint at Iliffe Press that I remember the very first time in my life I became seriously drunk. One night, I was invited to a staff drinks party to celebrate something or other. I was still only sixteen and I ended up drunk on port. Port! Apparently, I started performing outrageous songs and impressions standing on a table, and I can just about remember dancing with the managing director's secretary, who was very pretty. Unfortunately I became so ill that I ended up, literally, under the table. I still don't know exactly how I made it home. I was in serious disgrace by Monday.

I stayed at Iliffe Press for a while until my time-keeping became very erratic. I had to be in by nine o'clock every morning and I was always arriving at twenty past or half past nine. I would offer to make up the time in my lunch hour, but of course I never did so, because I was always down the pub with everybody else. Eventually I was sacked.

Next I went to work as an assembly-line labourer in a Morphy Richards factory that supplied high street stores with electrical goods like irons and kettles. Our factory was in St Mary's Cray, much closer to my home.

At the end of the day, I would be really black and grimy, covered in oil, and would need to take a shower. I used to love mucking around in the washrooms, swapping people's clothes over, or removing people's locker keys so that they couldn't fetch their clothes out after their shower. I messed about as much as I could. Then one day, as I was having a shower I suddenly sensed that something was going to happen. I looked up and saw six beefy guys all lined up. They said they had had enough of my practical jokes and that they were going to throw me out of the shower room – naked. At that moment my whole body was all greased up with this thick, green Swarfega. In a flash it crossed my mind that I might as well join in the fun. So I just charged at them, into this massive mangle of flesh. I managed to somehow wriggle right through the scrum and I eeled my way through and emerged the other side. Then they regrouped menacingly in a line by the shower-room door. To dodge them again, I leaped up on to a bench, stark bollock naked, and sneered at them, 'Ha, ha, ha!'

They just stood there, with their arms folded going, 'Haaa, haaa, haaa!' back.

And suddenly, I just turned round and received a shock. What I hadn't realised was that it was now eight o'clock in the evening and the entire night shift of four hundred women was just coming into the factory. Four hundred women waiting at their benches for their machines to start. Four hundred women staring at me. Suddenly, this enormous cheer went out. It was as if a riot had broken out.

Even through the green Swarfega they could see my blushes. The worst part came the following day when I returned for the morning shift. I had to clock on before eight o'clock and, of course, those very same four hundred women were still on the assembly lines ready to clock off. I had to walk in between lines of women screaming and jeering at me with remarks which were very funny but unrepeatable.

I had been working for about half an hour that morning when I was called in to the office by my bosses and summarily sacked. They said my behaviour was a disgrace. I had disrupted work and they couldn't allow it. I thought it was slightly unfair because, I pleaded, it was only a bit of innocent mischief that had misfired. But they would not listen. So I returned to the production line gutted and said, 'Thanks guys! I've just been sacked.' My workmates were rather crestfallen and so talked to the bosses on my behalf. I hung around rather nervously but the shop steward soon returned and told me that although they had explained that this was just a lark, the management remained unmoved. So I just went home.

The next day, I received a telephone call saying they had reconsidered their decision. Apparently, in my absence, the workforce had raised a petition to say they believed mine was a really unfair dismissal. Instead the management ended up suspending me for three days and after that I was able to return to work and reclaim my job. When I clocked in on my first shift after my suspension, I was greeted by this almighty cheer from the women. Thereafter I became known among the workforce by a new nickname. 'Oh look,' they'd cry, when I arrived for work, 'there goes The Phantom Flasher!' I remained with the company for about a further year before I was sacked again, this time for poor time-keeping.

About this time, I often went to Sidcup and drank in a pub in the high street called the Black Horse. It was there that I made loads of friends, friends that I have kept to this day. A few of us were keen on football and we formed a team which played in a local Sunday league. I don't think we ever actually managed to win a match but we used to play every week. We were always still drunk from the all-night party the night before, so I tried to register us with the Football Association under what I thought was the very appropriate name of the Sidcup Hiccups. Sadly, the FA would have none of it. They refused the name, which I thought was a bit mean.

I went through a series of different jobs, taking anything that paid me a wage. I used to deliver metal to Wales in a lorry. I would hire trucks and do deliveries of metal bearings all over the country. I also became a labourer at the Tip Top Bakeries in St Mary Cray, working at the ovens, which was seriously hard work. I toiled away for hours every day, taking the giant baking trays out of huge ovens and lifting enormous lids off them. Then I kneaded the bread into rolls and put the trays on to the conveyor belts. One of my jobs was to make French rolls, which required a certain amount of skill, actually, scooping up two pieces of dough, rolling them into two pipes, and then, a pipe in each hand, flicking them towards each other in a circular motion, bringing your wrists round to wrap the bread round like a plait. It needed a real knack, but it was mindbogglingly boring! So, to make things more interesting, I used to make rude rolls! I'd send down the line a long, unmistakably phallic piece of bread with two little round bits at the end. I also used to load the dough with different items, so that when people sliced open their bread, they would find sweets, or hidden messages such as: 'Help! I am being held prisoner.'

I bought my first car, a Ford Consul, when I was seventeen. That year I also had a girlfriend for whom I had developed very affectionate feelings. Part of me didn't want to become sexually involved with her, because I actually felt it was unkind to ruin the romantic side of our relationship, but I still had lusty aspirations and I certainly was no saint. Our relationship began after a friend of hers put the word around that she wanted to go out for a drink with me. So I took her for a drink and, after the pub, I drove out to some woods in South London behind Crystal Palace, where I parked the car. My enthusiastic fumblings were greeted with much appreciation and my Ford Consul allowed me to wave goodbye to childhood. I remember thinking that I'd finally grown into a man. I'm afraid I wasn't particularly attracted to this girl. But I was very grateful to her, and on reflection it was very pleasurable. And it happened in the front of my good old Ford Consul. Well, in the back too, and all over the place really. Let's just say we tested the suspension fully. After that day, she was always ringing me up and chasing me. But I just avoided her until she gave up, as my motives were lust, not romance.

After my next job, as a live-in barman in Roehampton, South-West London, I returned to live with my mother, and eventually I found work at Queen Mary's Hospital in Sidcup. Queen Mary's is an interesting building, originally opened for soldiers in the First World War and later expanded to accommodate other injured military personnel. The place was never properly designed, but just mushroomed, its various buildings spreading out all over the place. Wards were scattered everywhere, so that patients had to travel long distances between them. My first job at the hospital was as a 'physio porter', which was considered a plum job by other porters because you were always surrounded by pretty physiotherapists. Physios were often girls from comfortable families who wanted respectable jobs.

Back in those days, PR wasn't an option, so physiotherapy was the job to have!

I used to exercise the patients. and as part of my duties I also used to give them hot wax baths. Every day, I would walk with them, become friendly with a few of them and generally take care of their needs. Many stroke patients were sent to us and I remember fondly one old patient called Mr Plant, who lived on his own, so I used to go to his home at weekends and weed his garden for him, then just sit and drink coffee with him. I even spent one Christmas with him because he had nobody else.

It wasn't easy to transport patients from casualty or X-ray, or to different departments spread around the hospital. There were all sorts of 'trails' through the vast grounds and many of them ran over hills which became rally tracks as patients sat in their wheelchairs while we raced them. There were two routes to X-ray, and if we needed to take two patients down there, I'd push one and another porter the other. We would stand at the top of the hill and shout across, 'Go!' and see who could make it there the fastest. The patients used to stick their legs out, rigid with fear, although we had assured them we wouldn't go fast before we launched off. I'd stand on the back of the wheelchair as we sped down the hill, accelerating with my feet off the ground, and steering just by shifting my weight.

Hospitals offer ample opportunities for romance and I fell head over heels in love with a German nursing auxiliary called Helga, who had come over to improve her English with friends and shared a flat with them in the hospital grounds. Helga was very beautiful, extremely intelligent and bright, and above all, she was exceptionally well read. I used to make excuses to go over to her ward and chat and finally we started dating. There was a slight age gap – I was eighteen and she was twenty-five.

The first time I kissed her, she was leaning against a wall.

I eased up to her slowly and eventually moved in to kiss her. I closed my eyes and ended up kissing the wall because she had moved away! She was different from other girls I had dated and had flings with. And she was stunning. I had dated a few girls before this time, and I had sown my wild oats. Although I don't see myself as a particularly attractive person, I was always a success with the opposite sex and was never short of a girlfriend. To this day, I have always been romantic at heart.

While I was still working as a hospital porter, I also took a night job repossessing cars. This isn't a very pleasant way to earn a living but it paid – when I delivered the car. I usually worked at night, which was the best time to collect. I'd be given the name and address of somebody who hadn't kept up with their payments and I simply had to go and fetch the car. You have to work in pairs when repossessing cars because someone has to drive back the vehicle you have travelled in, and my colleague was a guy named Mike whom I used to share a flat with. We became pals, though a few years later, he was convicted and jailed for murder following a brawl outside a bar in Greece.

People were very clever about where they parked their cars. If we had an address and the make and registration number of the car, we would often drive to the house and no car would be found. We'd have to cruise around, and would often find the car lurking in someone else's driveway, or hidden around the back. Mike and I had a number of duplicate keys but sometimes they wouldn't work when we tried to start up the engine, so we'd have to break into the car and start it up. Turning the key in the ignition was always a frightening and anxious moment, because most of the people on the rough council estates where we ended up were pretty handy at taking care of themselves, and friends of theirs would also look out for them. I was in constant fear of people thinking that I was stealing their car, which in one sense we were, but I thought repossession was a politer way of describing it.

I once became stuck in a car at one o'clock in the morning on a council estate near Rochester. I was trying to start the engine and Mike was on the bike waiting to drive off. Suddenly I noticed Mike flashing me and I saw this brute was hurtling towards me. Boy, was he mad! There was no way I could make it across the forecourt to Mike. The car was locked from the inside but I still couldn't start it up. Meanwhile, the brute was outside, banging on the door. Bang, bang, bang! He couldn't break in, so he went away and came back with a brick and smashed the driver's window. I was terrified he was going to kill me. Desperately I tried to start the engine again. At the very last minute, with the shattered window splintering glass fragments all over me, the car finally started. I drove off at top speed and with a screech of burned tyres, I managed to escape. That was a very hairy moment.

I didn't really like doing the job, although I did enjoy the excitement and thrill of our commando raids. On one hilarious occasion, I completely messed up by taking away the wrong car, obviously a fairly unclever thing to do. There were two almost identical cars and I simply drove the wrong one away. Mike quickly flashed me down and told me my mistake. So we had to go back. I put the wrong car back, and then I took the right one.

I became hopelessly romantically involved with Helga. We went on a wonderful holiday in a gypsy caravan in Ireland and the trip left me with a life-long passion for the country. One day Helga left her handbag on the table in a tiny pub, and we had travelled on for hours and many miles before she realised her mistake. When we went back, there was the bag, still on the table.

Helga was visiting Britain on a fixed-term study period to learn English and her trip eventually came to an end. It broke my heart, although she wasn't really as passionate about me as I was about her. She was older and more sophisticated. I was a hospital porter, while she had grand ambitions to be an actress; her father was a doctor from a very well-to-do family. Importantly she revived my great, innate interest in books. It sounds absurd but she seemed so cultured to me back then. I came from a council estate and had been to a secondary modern school and spent a great deal of my time in the pub. And then suddenly this woman walked into my life, talking about literature, music, the arts and films in a way I'd never heard before. Helga fostered not only a romantic awakening, but also touched parts that nobody else had. I felt I naturally veered towards a richer, deeper side of life, and I liked to always examine things that other people took for granted.

I didn't take Helga for granted but it still knocked me for six when, one day, she announced that it was time for her to leave England and return to Germany. I pledged faithfully that I would follow her over and find work there. From all the extra work and long hours I had been putting in at this time, I actually had just about enough money to afford the trip to Germany. I was determined to stay by Helga's side, even though she insisted I didn't have to follow her.

I was all set to leave when catastrophe struck and I was suddenly admitted to hospital myself. The doctors thought I had meningitis at first because I was suffering from really severe headaches. Helga left while I was in hospital, and I was devastated. It turned out I was suffering from a very severe bout of sinusitis, caused through lack of sleep. I really had been burning the candle at both ends for a very long time.

After a week in hospital I slowly recovered and returned home to nurse my sinusitis and my broken heart. I had always known that Helga wasn't going to be in England for ever and I'd also always had it in the back of my mind that I would follow her to Germany. Nevertheless, her decision to leave England was more of a surprise than I expected, so when I came out of hospital, I did many more odd jobs to replenish my finances and pay for my visit to Helga. I worked as a barman and when I'd saved enough, I chucked in both my jobs, as porter and barman, packed my bag and hitch-hiked.

Helga had returned with her flatmate, a girl called Spatz and Helga was staying with her in Hamburg, so that was where I hitch-hiked. I had some money saved up but first of all I had to find myself a place to live. I took digs in the middle of Hamburg, near a huge lake called the Alster, not unlike the Serpentine in London. My room was just off a place called Mittelweg, or Middle Way, in a one-room apartment shared with fourteen Portuguese and Spanish guys. Obviously the accommodation was cheap and there were bunk beds, and we had to share one bathroom. All the others were working illegally in Hamburg, as waiters, in factories and in shops. I intended to do the same.

I remember coming back one night very late to find one of these guys sleeping in my bed. He looked so comfortable tucked up there at two o'clock in the morning so, rather than wake the poor sod, I decided to leave him and slept on the floor that night. In the morning, they woke me up because they were leaving for work very early and they saw what I'd done. They were very impressed, just because I hadn't woken up this Portuguese guy. We became firm friends and they sorted me a job working in a restaurant. I couldn't do much because I couldn't speak German so I washed up and cleared dishes. But I got on like a house on fire with my Portuguese chums. I couldn't speak Portuguese and none of them could speak English either, so we communicated through sign language.

I spent most of my free time looking for another job, and eventually, I found one in a car-breaker's yard, humping and shifting broken cars in a fork-lift truck. My new boss

41

was a man of mystery and a bit of a villain, and all sorts of shady characters used to walk in and out. Because I didn't have a work permit I was working there illegally and I remember arriving one day to find an empty police car parked outside. The officers were inside interviewing the boss, who shot me a glance when the police weren't looking. I understood the message right away and scarpered. When I went back later he apologised. 'Sorry, friend,' he said. 'The police told me you don't have a work permit, so you'll have to go.' So that was that. Another job bit the dust.

I did all these odd jobs because I was passionately in love with Helga. I had imagined we had a future together although I don't think she saw things the way I did. Around that time, The Beatles were a big thing back in Britain and so anything English was very 'in' throughout Europe. I had reckoned that I would be able to capitalise on this in Germany. My English appeal was bound to lead to offers of interesting and rewarding jobs. I could make enough money for Helga and I to be together. But it was a real struggle, scouring newspapers and attending interviews. I didn't speak German so I could only apply for menial jobs, and over and over again people would ask me the same question, 'Do you have a work permit?' I'd have to say no and so I would be rejected. Money became tight.

Then one fine day, I struck lucky with a truly wonderful job in the city centre of Hamburg. This time I'd told the authorities that I *did* have a work permit and that there was no problem with it. I said I'd just lost the document, and a copy was still coming through. The job was as a lavatory attendant.

I had higher aspirations in life, of course, but public lavatories in Germany are run on military discipline. A guy in uniform came round to inspect them and he was like the classic regimental sergeant-major back home in Britain. He would march up and down, running his fingers along all the surfaces to ensure there was no dirt. My job entailed having to make sure that there was enough loo paper and soap. I also had to clean the floor and taps. My toilet had to be kept immaculately clean and washed at all times. And it was!

This job, probably my very first position in authority, provided me with a fabulous daily opportunity for mischief making and practical joking. Someone has left behind a small radio and, on quiet days, I used to play music very loudly, then rush outside to entertain passing pedestrians by juggling toilet brushes in time with the music.

Inside, I also kept a little teapot-cum-kettle, which I put to good use by using it to block up all the toilets and urinal bowls. I'd empty the yellow-brown contents of my teapot, which looked like something else, (I promise you it was only cold tea!), then I would stuff my teabags down the toilets to block them up. I made doubly sure the drains were out of order by stuffing in Cellophane from discarded cigarette packets. when all the cubicles were safetly blocked, I'd pour in my tea. It looked very realistic, I can assure you! The men would rush in, desperate for a pee, and move from one urinal to the next trying to find one they could use. They found the toilets were blocked too. When they couldn't relieve themselves, they naturally rushed over to me to complain. And I'd just shrug my shoulders and say: 'Sorry, full up. Full up!' And then the men used to run out with their legs crossed.

The other way I had tremendous fun was with the toilet rolls. Sometimes, I used to arrange it that the toilets ran out of paper, just to force people to come to me. They would shout at me in German and then I could claim not to understand a word of what they were saying. The aper they used was awful, high gloss and extremely uncomfortable. But my toilet rolls were full of fun!

I liked to load various bits and pieces into the rolls. You will always find flies and spiders in a toilet, especially in the summer. I'd swat some, then, when no one was looking, I took a toilet roll, a pen or a knife, and slid in a spider or a fly between the sheets of paper in the roll. When the roll came to be used by someone in my cubicle, they would reach this bit of paper and the insect would drop out. Marvellous! A big reaction was guaranteed. I would also load the rolls with coins and hear them tinkle on the floor.

Talking of coins, for a joke, I also used to drop German Mark coins into the urinals, just to see if anybody would take them out. And they always did! I used to flick one silver coin in, worth about ten pence, the guys would come in for a pee, and sooner or later, one of them would furtively look from side-to-side, then actually dip his hand into the urine-filled toilet to take the coin. Deary me!

One of my favourite tricks was to quickly enter a cubicle beside someone else. Then I would start making terrible noises. This trick would always work especially well if two people were already sitting down in cubicles on either side. I would close my door and then start making horrendous grunting and farting sounds. 'Brrrrrrrrrrrrrrrrrrrrrrrr!' and 'Uuuuuuuuughhhhhhh!' The sounds would just go on and on and on. For a great variation on this one, I also used an old Fairy Liquid bottle with a large nozzle. I would empty all the washing-up liquid from it, then fill it right to the top with water. Again, when the moment was right, I'd nip into the middle cubicle with men either side of me, and start slowly emptying the contents of the bottle into the pan. It made the sound of peeing, but the pee would go on, and on, and on, and on, and on. When I'd finished, I nipped out before the other guys and went to sit back down on my chair. When they came out, they were wide-eyed and would look each other up and down suspiciously.

A traditional German, the uniformed inspector always came to my toilet at exactly the same time. So I always knew when to expect him and there was little danger of my ever being found out. Eventually, presumably after some complaints, I was caught. The inspector came in with my wages and announced that he had discovered there was no work permit. I had to leave immediately. I waved goodbye to a wonderful career.

I continued to find odd jobs here and there for a while after that, but I slowly lost touch with Helga, who told me she wanted to start a career as an actress in radio, which she was very interested in. Sadly, I saw less and less of her. Meanwhile, I was struggling just to keep my head above water and stay out of trouble.

Then, one day I was stopped by the police, who wanted to know where I was living, what I was doing and how I was supporting myself. I didn't have the right answers. They said I was in Germany illegally, without a work permit, and took me back to my digs, where I gathered my belongings. The police marked my passport and ordered me to leave the country. What really pissed me off was that, in order to be expelled, I had to buy a rail ticket. That was the tough one. I thought I could manage with just telling them, 'Okay, I'm going,' then hitch to another town. But although I had next to no money they still forced me to buy the ticket. A funny little guy in uniform had to stand on the railway station platform and wave me goodbye.

Eventually I went back to selling advertising. I was nineteen when I worked for Mercury Publications in London, selling ad space. The job wasn't up to much but, once again, I found time for some fabulous pranks and practical jokes. And I re-established contact with my old school friend Derek Dowsett.

Our offices were in Waterloo Road, opposite Waterloo Station, and it was my job to sell space for new magazines like *Computer Weekly* and *Data Week*. This was 1967 and they were the first computer magazines to be published.

They contained editorial features but they were mainly bought by readers who desired to be recruited as systems analysts or programmers. Back then, this was a new and burgeoning industry.

I say I '*worked*' there but who actually *works* in an office? There were good and bad periods for selling advertising. We had 'down time' during the lunch hour, when it was always difficult to contact people on the phone. Our offices were situated across the street from the station. Just down the road the late Great Train Robber Buster Edwards later set up his flower stall.

I liked to play games. Directly opposite our offices were two public telephone kiosks, on either side of the street but in full view from our office. One lunchtime, I went down and noted the telephone numbers of both of the phones. I was then armed to play various tricks. With my most regular one, I just rang the number until somebody passing by stopped to pick it up. In my happiest voice, I would announce, 'Hi, congratulations. I'm calling from the *Evening Standard* and you have a chance to win £1000. All you have to do is to locate Chalkie.' And I'd continue, 'Now, you are on Waterloo Road. You have just sixty seconds to locate Chalkie.' At that point I'd look up the road to see who was walking towards the kiosk, then add, 'But you must say the password absolutely right. If it isn't absolutely right, the person you think is Chalkie will deny that they are Chalkie and you will not win the money. Do you under-stand?' The budding winner would reply, 'Yes.' I would then provide them with the most ridiculous passwords. 'You'll have to go up to Chalkie and say, "The penguin's feet are blue but the beer is good." Have you understood that?' And they'd reply, 'Yes, yes. "The penguin's feet are blue but the beer is good." And then I'd continue, 'Okay, approaching you shortly will be . . .' and at this point, I would look up the street and describe the first stranger I spotted. 'He'll be wearing a white mac with a brown Trilby hat and carrying a briefcase. You must grab him, but remember – if you don't say the password absolutely right, he will deny he is Chalkie.'

People used to come dashing out of the phone box and grab the passer-by as we watched from our window. They'd blurt out, 'The penguin's feet are blue but the beer was good. You're Chalkie and I demand my £1000.' Of course, the disbelieving man in the Trilby would say, 'What!? What the hell are you talking about?' Then the first person would repeat the password. When that failed to impress, they would often grab the person and not let them go, because they thought they must have delivered the phrase slightly wrongly, and they would yank them back to the box. They'd come back on the line and say to me, 'Look, this Chalkie person is right here and he's denying it's him.' I'd reply, 'Ah, you obviously didn't get the message right. What did you say?' They'd tell me, and I'd reply, 'Ah, that wasn't exactly correct. Try variations.'

My office was located on the first floor, with windows immediately above the street, so we had a close and clear view of all these proceedings. There was a bus shelter bench next to the phones and, at other times, if I saw a girl sitting there, I used to try to make a passing guy pick up the phone. When a young man stopped to pick up the receiver in the kiosk, I'd say, 'Look, I'm really sorry to do this to you but I've just had a big row with my girlfriend. I know you're in a public call box but just a few seconds ago she put the phone down on me so I know she must be there. She can't be far away. She must be around there somewhere. Please help me. I was hoping she would pick up the phone again. Can you see her? She's wearing . . .' and I would describe the girl sitting on the bench. 'Would you please go up to her and say, "Jimmy really loves you. Please will you forgive him because he's on the phone now."'

Eventually my boss found out what I was up to and, guess what – I got the sack again. So, I decided to hit the road once more.

On my next trip hitching back to Germany, I had a gun pointed at me, which is something I will never forget. I was still trying to mend bridges and work things out with Helga, who was then in Munich. As I'd done Hamburg job-wise I decided to go down there too. My luck might improve, I reckoned.

The moment I chose to go travelling coincided precisely with when most of the students of Europe were also on the road. Hitching in Europe was difficult at the best of times and now I was right up against it. At an Autobahn stopover point I met a hiker dressed in full Scottish regalia. He wore kilt, socks and tartan jacket and even carried a set of bag-pipes. Because I could see he was Scottish, I went over to say hello. To my surprise, he turned out to be a Cockney. I said, 'You don't sound very Scottish.' 'Naah mate.' he replied, ''course I'm not Sco'ish. But this is the best gimmick I know for hitch-hiking. The longest I've ever waited for a lift is about ten minutes because people are so curious.' I said, 'Do you mean to tell me you *put on* a Scottish accent?' He replied, 'Naah, course I don't. But I've invented a few Sco'ish relations. I've an Uncle Rob Roy.' It was a wonder-ful technique.

When hitching, the most important thing was not to end up stuck on an Autobahn stopover. You needed to make it on to a major feed road. One day in Cologne about twenty hitch-hikers were already waiting on the feed road when I turned up. I thought to myself, 'Oh, no!' because there was this unwritten rule of the road whereby you would take your place in line so that the person closest to the exit picked up the first lift. In those days and drivers were generous so even if sometimes you were stuck for hours and hours you usually didn't have to wait too long. But this time, the huge queue of hitch-hikers made me think I'd had it, so I walked right past them and went down on to the motorway itself. I didn't want to miss the cars and I thought perhaps the drivers would assume I was the first in the queue. What I didn't know was, just around the corner, hidden behind some bushes, were the Autobahn police.

Obviously it was illegal, and rightly so, to hitch-hike on the motorways themselves. A police car came round the corner, saw me, and two policemen jumped out. They told me I had to go back. 'This is the Autobahn,' the young policeman said to me. 'No, it's not. This is the Einfahrt, the entrance, not the Autobahn,' says I. The policeman repeated, 'This is the Autobahn.' I had a stand-up row with this young policeman, who eventually started pushing me around. He shouted, 'Step back!' But I insisted, 'No, no, no. I'm staying here.' I knew that if I went back I would never be offered a lift.

The policeman finally lost his patience, and pulled a gun on me! And again he said, 'Step back!' He pointed the gun straight at me at arm's length and shouted again, 'Step back!'

I looked at the gun. I was shocked and terrified. But I also thought these were real bully-boy tactics, and something inside me just snapped. I said, 'I am staying here.'

By now the policeman and his buddy had really had their fill of my arguing. They physically picked me up, opened their car door and threw me in the back. The rear section of their vehicle had grilles on it and I was squeezed behind them. Then they drove me to a special exit, only about two hundred yards down the road, straight into their police station.

The scene was like something out of a movie. Squads of hefty, uniformed policemen stomped around in their heavy boots, and the atmosphere was really smoky. They threw me into a cell and clanged the door shut. Then, after a couple of hours, I was brought out and hauled in front of a police chief. He said, 'You were trespassing on the motorway and you have to pay a fine. You are fined on the spot.'

I said, 'I'm sorry, but I don't have the money.' And again I started arguing. Now, the guy started screaming at me. 'You will go back to the cell!' he shrieked. 'You will do zis and zat . . . We will deport you . . .' and who knows what else. But I was having none of it, demanding that someone fetch the British Consul and all sorts of other things. If I'd had any sense, I would have done as I was told on the Autobahn. But no, no, no. I just had to argue, didn't I?

Then the police chief drew a gun on me! I stood my ground. I thought, 'I haven't done anything that serious, he can't possibly pull a gun on me. It must be illegal to draw a gun in an unthreatening situation.' And they just muttered on. Finally, they grabbed hold of me, one on each limb, and violently hurled me out of the police station. I rolled when I hit the ground and they threw my bag after me, shouting, 'There! Last chance.' The irony was I had to walk back up the road, where a long line was still waiting for a lift. I stuck my thumb out and a car picked me up immediately. The driver presumably assumed I must have been the first in the queue. And I wasn't – I was the last. The lift took me a couple of hundred miles. Despite all that fuss, I was on my way!

At one stage, I spent a couple of nights sleeping rough in a telephone box in deep snow because I had nowhere else to stay and no money. Helga was also due to be there but she hadn't arrived yet. I knew nobody, and the only place I could find any shelter in the suburbs was this telephone box. To my horror, when I arrived in Munich it turned out that Helga was only visiting for a couple of days so I only saw her for about an hour. I was really upset. I knew some friends from the Royal College of Music were on a trip to Austria at that time. One was Geoff Westley, who, in fact, would later become the musical director of the Bee Gees and David Essex. He also worked with Kiki Dee, and was a very talented musician in his own right. He had organised a trip for everyone to visit Salzburg and the city's music festival. I decided to try to link up with them and hitched from Hamburg to just outside Salzburg, which is a fair old distance. It took me three days. And the weather was freezing.

I finally managed to link up with the students from the Royal College of Music, walking in on them one morning as a surprise. I stayed with them for about five days, hidden in their hostel until they went home. Then I landed a job in a woodcutter's yard, humping wood and stacking logs and timbers. I didn't stay there for long.

Next, from Munich, I headed down to Italy via Salzburg. I hitched over the border easily enough and then went down to Ravenna on the Adriatic. I wanted to go there because Oscar Wilde, who has always been one of my idols, had written about Ravenna and I have always loved Italians. I fell in with some Africans selling beads and watches, real cut-throats. I didn't do very well working with them. They gave me some stock and I started wandering round the beach, until I was pulled by the police and kicked out again.

I hitched from there through France and did some fruit-picking as I was now very short of money. Then I went down to Spain. I would meet people on the road and they would tell me where to find work.

I was nineteen or twenty at the time, and I was very excited by the lifestyle I was leading. I genuinely loved it, despite all the discomfort and risk, despite the fact that I had no money and was always scrounging. I kept thinking, 'Oh, something's going to turn up ...' It was very Pickwickian. I met some extraordinary people on the road. In the South of France, everybody carried guitars and books of poetry, and were very beatnik. I discovered that

51

the French could create food out of anything and make it taste delicious. I learned that they loved to talk. I sampled the French pace of life and I loved to simply walk along the roads beside vast fields of sunflowers and corn. I really loved it. It was better than selling advertising space!

There were lessons of kindness. When people would help me out for no special reason, I could see for myself that it was simply a case of people purely being kind, charitable and thoughtful. People would offer me their barns to sleep in. In return I'd do odd jobs. But I continually had to move on because the police would be on my back. I had no work permit. I had no money. And so I was considered a bum. I was thrown out of France without ceremony, my name was put on the register of undesirables and I was told that if I was found in the country within forty-eight hours of my expulsion, I would be arrested for vagrancy. Indeed, I was arrested for vagrancy a couple of times.

When I fancied a rest from all this bumming around, I came back to England and found a flat in Sidcup. I landed another job working as a porter in an Orpington hospital, where there were frequent opportunities to earn overtime. I was drinking in the pub one night with my friend Derek. 'When are we going back? he asked. 'You promised that I could come with you the next time you went over.'

So Derek and I bought a second-hand Austin Champ jeep and headed for Germany and this time The Beatles were on hand to help us out more obviously. We just *had* to obtain work permits, so we went to the immigration office to apply for permits. We said that we had jobs promised to us and we needed permits. The official asked me, 'Your name is Beadle? Are you related to The Beatles?' I said, 'Oh, yes, yes.' I said that Paul McCartney was my cousin and that they took their name from our family name, just adding a 'T'. This official became terribly excited. He produced various documents and it turned out that he was the man who gave The Beatles their first German work permit. He had kept it – and their signatures – as a matter of pride, in his desk. I said, 'Oh yes, my cousin.' The official was so completely bamboozled, so that he simply gave us the stamp.

We didn't have much money when we reached Hamburg but we managed to secure a comfortable flat. We started hunting for jobs right away and, because we were English in the era of The Beatles, we found work in a night club, where the owner was very excited about having two English disc jockeys on the staff. Derek had everything going for him. He was very good looking and became the star jock. I usually had to do all the clearing up and delivering the records. But while it seemed glamorous, it was actually very poorly paid. We had a bit to drink, but that was the only perk. To save money on petrol, and because the Austin Champ really used to guzzle fuel, we always used to walk to work and back.

In a very minor way, we enjoyed celebrity. Derek was always very successful with women, but I met one or two girls as well. We both had a few women to keep us fed and watered during this time.

Late one night we were coming home from the club when suddenly we saw a big commotion and lights in the distance. It turned out to be a location for the production of a feature film. We recognised Kurt Jurgens, who was then one of Germany's biggest and most glamorous film stars. He was shooting a scene in a large apartment block, and people kept walking up to the door. Derek and I watched from a distance, fascinated by the whole process. It was about three o'clock in the morning but we didn't mind – we were having fun. As it was a night-time shoot, it had an enormous number of arc lights. The crew would rehearse, then the director would call out, '*Gunther – licht!*' and the whole street would light up.

The lighting man, whose name was presumably Gunther, was some way out of sight, sitting at the controls. Again, we heard, '*Gunther – licht!*' The lights snapped on for about twenty seconds. Then they'd film a retake. The director would shout, '*Gunther – licht!*'

After a few minutes I realised we could have a bit of a lark. So we hid in the bushes near where they were rehearsing, and I shouted out at the top of my voice, '*Gunther?*'and a little voice would go, '*Ja?*' and I shouted '*Licht!*' Zap! Everything lit up. Then the director shouted back in an angry voice, '*Gunther – nicht licht!*' We did this, I promise you, about twelve times, tears streaming down our faces. We were never rumbled. Every time our friend Gunther put the arc lights back on, the director came storming out yelling, '*Gunther – nicht licht!*' They never sussed it.

Derek had an enormous appetite, but we had no money. We used to walk home across the Alster Park, where Hamburg pedestrians could enjoy the gardens and the *lake* right in the heart of the city. Derek would suffer these gourmet cuisine pangs and, one night, he suddenly had a passion for duck, announcing there were ducks in the park and he wanted to go and find one to eat. It made sense. Catching a duck on foot is quite a difficult feat. But catching one at three o'clock in the morning is even more of a task. Ducks are clever little creatures, who look at you in a funny way and make very appealing noises, but they sure can shift when they need to. Derek and I grabbed these two huge broken branches and we spent about an hour running around, trying to wallop a duck. As it was dark and we had had far too much to drink, we were tripping over and these ducks were getting the better of us every time. Eventually we designed a strategy. Apache-like, we would corral the poor innocent duck. Derek chanted to himself, 'I *must* have duck. I *must* have duck.'

Eyeing this poor little duck, we began to approach it very slowly, until gradually we had it trapped in a corner. Derek and I had these two enormous branches raised above our heads, like Anne Boleyn's executioner, and this little duck sat there in the corner, peering at us under the bright moon. The poor animal is standing there waiting for something to happen. It started making these rather sad little last quacks, 'Pwp, pwp.' Eventually, I turned to Derek and I said, 'I can't do it. I just can't do it.' He said, 'I *must* have duck.' I said, 'I *can't* do it.' He said, 'You've got to.' I said, 'I don't *want* duck and I don't *want* to kill this little fella. No! Derek, I'm having nothing to do with this.' I walked away and sat down on a park bench round the corner of a tree and waited for the final quack.

After about ten minutes, Derek came back with a terrible expression on his face. There was a deathly hush. A long pause. Then he looked at me and said, 'I just can't do it!' And we both sat there, two hulking guys, clutching two great big sticks, one of us starving for a bit of duck meat. Then to cap it all, this little duck had the *nerve* to stick its head round the corner and then just come waddling past us and away.

Despite the fact that we were regularly fed by our various girlfriends, Derek's huge appetite cost us a fortune, and we were forced to adopt desperate measures. We even ended up breaking the law, which is not something I would encourage, in hindsight. But when you're desperate, you are desperate.

At the end of our street, which was close to the centre of Hamburg, was a large supermarket, where we went on daily 'shopping sprees'. The only difference between most people's shopping sprees and ours was that most people *paid* for them. Our technique was very simple. We would go in and I would start entertaining all the customers. The regulars all knew us because we would often go in and buy

Derek's milk or bread, and I would always muck about with the other shoppers in the store. I used to waltz the women up and down the aisles and juggle and perform various stunts. While I held their attention and they were laughing and enjoying my entertainment, Derek would meanwhile poach what he needed. At the given signal, telling me that he'd finished his filching and had bagged what he wanted, Derek would leave, and I would just buy the bread. It was a simple matter of misdirection.

On one occasion, Derek turned round to me and said, 'I *must* have chicken!' I said, 'Oh no, not again?' He replied, 'Yes, I need the chicken. I need the protein.' So off we went to the supermarket. As usual, I started prancing and leaping around while Derek headed towards the freezer cabinet. I was really having a whale of a time as Derek stuffed the chicken down his shirt, under his jacket, but this time I was *really* enjoying my leaping around and I must have got a bit carried away. The shop was full by now, and I was doing headstands and balancing acts, singing and dancing with the ladies, forming a conga. But I forgot to look out for Derek's signal. Now! Now! Now! I spotted him once, out of the corner of my eye, and he seemed really frantic, so I signalled back, 'Okay, any minute,' but then I forgot and carried on.

Eventually I came to my senses and turned round to see Derek throwing daggers at me, so I quickly distracted everyone and he went out into the street. I bought bread and eggs and raced back to the flat, to find Derek in agony. 'What's the matter?' I enquired. He had shoved the chicken down his shirt on to his chest and, because it was frozen, it had stuck solid to his skin. To prove it, he stood up and the chicken stuck fast to his chest! I poured cold water on him. We spent the rest of the day thawing this chicken off his chest. He was going mad. What a laugh! Eventually, we peeled it off and poor Derek was left with this huge strawberry scar, right in the middle of his torso. The chicken had the last laugh. Derek had been looking forward to a hearty chicken dinner but after we had delicately removed it we found that it had gone bad. Derek wanted to take it back to the supermarket to complain! I had to explain to him that, in the circumstances, that was not really an option . . .

Another bit of mischief we engineered is something else I am not proud of. Derek and I had no money and we used to walk through some wealthy Hamburg suburbs. Occasionally, people are foolish enough to leave their cars open, and sometimes, we would find one open. We weren't after car radios and we never nicked anything of value. We were only looking for parking money. Spare change left on a car dashboard was always useful. If we saw loose coins around, we would check the doors first, and if they were locked, you'd be surprised how many could be opened. I did already have the techniques available to me . . .

We had a great time in Hamburg but we were still very short of cash. Derek had family in Holland, so we decided to drive to Holland. We ended up in Amsterdam, but we couldn't work there. Derek's brother-in-law worked for an oil company in Holland and offered him a job on the North Sea rigs, so Derek decided to go back, and because we shared the Austin Champ jeep we both agreed to go back together. Derek went to the rigs and I went off to live in Brighton, but fully expected to continue travelling sometime soon. At the time, I didn't think the curtain was going to be drawn on this chapter in my life but in fact this marked the end of my travels.

By the end of the sixties, I had learned a great deal about independence, about different cultures and also, most importantly, about myself. I had learned about kindness and hardship. I had always felt like an outsider and travel confirmed that instinct. Travelling taught me to be resilient. I learned what it was like to have no food, no money, no work. I learned for the first time in my life what it was like to have no roof over my head, and no prospects. I slept in fields, in boiler rooms and telephone kiosks. It was not at all romantic or charming, and I was always expecting to be picked up for vagrancy at any second or to be chased out of the farm by some vicious dogs. But I wouldn't have missed my travels for all the tea in China.

Most people have a star hovering over them, although it's often shrouded in mist and cloud. But the star is still there. How their future pans out depends on whether people follow their star or not. I always secretly believed that my star was up there. Occasionally it would flash and lead me on. Every opportunity that presented itself to me, however humble or obscure, was a challenge. Following this star would often land me in unchartered territory. Life on the road was hard, but it toughened me up for the rough-and-tumble world in which I was about to move.

4

CRASH, BANG, WALLOP! WHAT A PICTURE!

When I returned home to Britain, the door of opportunity opened wide – but I didn't realise it was a *revolving* door! I had come back penniless. I went to live in central London with my Mum, who now had a flat in Semley Place, above Victoria bus station.

Derek's job on the rigs only lasted for a short time and he was soon back in London, where he had landed himself a job selling advertising space. He had a wonderfully flash new company car, and one day I went along with him on a business trip. We were driving out of Norfolk and, as we passed through Cambridge, I asked if I could take the wheel.

It was an absolutely perfect day. The sky was cloudless, beaming brilliant sunshine, so I decided to put Derek's car through its paces. We reached a long stretch of dual car-riageway. In the distance, a single-decker bus had started to come down the hill towards us, slowing and signalling that it was going to turn right and cut across my lane. I was probably doing about sixty-five miles per hour, getting closer and closer to the bus. I remember asking myself why he didn't pull over and wait. He had acres of time. He must have been day dreaming, because it gradually dawned on me that he was, in fact, going to pull across the two lanes right in front of us. Hurtling towards him, I hurriedly changed gear, going down into third, slammed my foot hard on the brakes, and turned the wheel to avoid the bus.

Our car just went into a tail spin. We were doing well over sixty when we hit the bus and the last thing I remember was going into slow motion, looking over my shoulder and seeing all these little faces peering at me in horror from inside the bus. I don't remember the impact but, some time afterwards, I woke up in a ditch and found people huddled all over me. It was the fire brigade. I heard someone shouting in surprise, 'He's alive!' I would have glass fragments coming out of me for the next year. It turned out that Derek had managed to scramble free and I had been left trapped inside. The firemen had to cut half the frame off to reach me because it was completely crushed. I kept apologising to Derek about the car.

They finally pulled me out and laid me down on the side of the road as they bandaged me up. I was in a terrible daze, with blood everywhere, and I felt an excruciating pain in my shoulder. Then a guy came up to me and said, 'Look, we can't book an ambulance but we've ordered a minicab. Will you be all right?' I mumbled back, 'Yeah, yeah.' So I just sat there for about fifteen minutes, watching tow trucks pulling away the wreckage. The car was a complete write-off.

When the minicab arrived, the driver had quite a broad accent and asked me, 'Where do you wanna go?' The people by the roadside told him to take me to Addenbrookes Hospital. So he helped me into the back of his car, while Derek stayed behind to talk to the police.

As we drove away, the minicab driver piped up, 'I say, I'm afraid I've been booked on another pick-up because I was called out here all of a sudden. It's this old lady. Do you mind if I pick her up too?' Still dazed, I said, 'No, no, fine.'

So, we drove deep into the countryside to find the house where this little old lady lived. Picture the scene: me, in enormous pain, bloodied, covered with glass splinters, my clothes ripped, arm in a temporary sling. When we eventually reached the old lady, she simply jumped in and sat down beside me. 'Ah, hello dear!' she said, and then proceeded to tell me her life story. I was in a real state but she didn't seem to notice. She just carried right on chatting away. 'Had an accident, eh? Oh, I had an accident once . . .' On and on she went. I was in no fit condition to respond. When we finally arrived at the entrance of the hospital, the cab driver stopped at the foot of the driveway leading to Addenbrookes. 'Would you mind jumping out here?' he asked. 'It's just that, if I go all the way up to the hospital entrance, it means I'll have to take a detour right round the one-way system. And then it'll take me extra time to drive back and I'm already a bit behind schedule.'

I climbed out of the car and somehow made it up to the casualty department. The nurses greeted me warmly: 'Ah, we've been expecting you!' They immediately laid me down on a stretcher, then, after a couple of minutes, Derek arrived. In those days Derek smoked pot and he always kept his miniature supply in a box of matches. He arrived at the hospital in the company of a policeman, who started asking me questions. While he was doing so, I asked if he minded me having a cigarette, because I used to smoke back then. Derek offered me one and lobbed me his box of matches. I knew what it contained! And right in front of me a policeman was chatting merrily away. I stared at Derek. He stared back at me. I thought, 'Thank you very much indeed!'

As they moved me off to see the doctors, I threw this box of matches into a cubicle where some other patient was lying because I didn't want to be caught in possession of it. I hasten to add that I didn't smoke pot. That wasn't my

61

scene. Nevertheless, I hope that guy in the cubicle had a good night on it!

It transpired that I had snapped my arm and my shoulder and I was kept in hospital for about three days. I had to take a heap of painkillers and, when I stood up, my right arm was hanging down to my knee, swinging loose. The hospital said there was nothing they could do. 'Shall I change all my suits, then?' I said, as a joke.

I went home to the flat in Victoria, which I had all to myself because my mum was away on holiday. I kept taking the painkillers and, after about three days, my local doctor sent me to Westminster Hospital, where I saw a specialist. They took me in the following day and pinned up the arm. I was sent to the orthopaedic ward, which had probably fourteen or fifteen patients. I got chatting to them all and made a few friends. On one occasion, we decided to see how much attention the doctors *really* paid us and I went round the ward and switched round everybody's charts, so that nobody had their correct chart clipped to their bed. Everybody agreed not to say anything.

The doctors breezed in, inspecting the clipboards hanging at the end of each bed. One by one, they met the patients. 'Ah-ha, Mr Jones. I see you are doing well. How's it going?' and so on. They went right through the entire ward, and they didn't once realise, not once in fifteen patients, that they were reading the wrong patient's charts. They just carried on, saying, 'Hello, how are we today?' looking at a chart and asking, 'So, how is the arm?' while in front of them the patient's *leg* would be in plaster.

After I recovered, I met up with my old friend Geoff Westley again. He lived in Chislehurst, which was a rather upper-class area of Kent. He played the piano and we produced a few charity gigs together, including an old time music hall charity show at Orpington Civic Hall, where as a young thrusting teenager I used to go ballroom dancing. I used to visit Geoff at the Royal College of Music and one day he introduced me to these two fellow students, who seemed very posh to me at the time, like most of the students there were. I asked them what they were doing and one replied, 'Oh, we're working on an opera.' They must have been all of about eighteen or nineteen. 'Oh yeah?' said I. 'Yes, it's a rock opera.' 'Ah ha,' said I. 'What's the storyline, then?' 'It's a rock opera about Jesus Christ.' 'Oh, yeah!' I thought they were a pair of rather stuck-up idiots but I carried on talking to them about their idea, which I thought was absolutely stupid. People were just going to laugh, I thought to myself, or all the religious groups would be up in arms. Also, I couldn't get my head around the concept of a rock opera. It seemed a contradiction in terms. I remember saying to Geoff afterwards, 'Hey, there's a couple of mugs!'

You've guessed their names by now – Andrew Lloyd Webber and Tim Rice. As they say in all the best biographies, the rest is history.

Geoff was working as a musician and had been offered a season down in Brighton. I rather fancied a change of scenery, and I'd always loved the seaside, so the prospect of living in Brighton suddenly appealed. In those days, I had all the freedom in the world just to go wherever whim or chance led me. As it was summer, the town was getting busy. The Brighton scene was bursting with young people, supposedly studying, but really just interested in going out and having a good time. The town had a large number of language schools catering for Continental students learning English. I would say that 80 per cent of these students were girls and at least 70 per cent were Scandinavian. So Brighton, during the summer, became a fabulous hunting ground for a lusty twenty-year-old like myself! Failure to score in Brighton in those days was something you could only really put down to lack of effort. The big question as far as I was concerned was how to meet these gorgeous people. I had a small problem – despite the presence of all these lovely ladies – I had no money!

In the face of adversity, not for the first time in my life, I came up with a scam. I decided to become a photographer. Simply carrying a camera allowed Geoff and I to chat up girls. I'd go up to a group of girls and say, 'Excuse me, would you mind if I took your photograph? You have great faces, and we are here scouting for an advertising agency.' And the girls would be terribly flattered by this and lap it up. If they became self-conscious, I'd use flattery to make them feel at their ease. I'd spin them a yarn about how attractive and unusual they were, and then get them to strike ridiculous poses, anything to show off their legs or their bust, or I'd ask them to blow a kiss into the lens. Of course, later on we'd end up enjoying a drink and having a good time, but of course, the irony was that there would never be any film in the camera! A few days later they would want the pictures but sadly, there *were* no pictures. Occasionally, we did put film in the camera, when we could afford one, but most of the time, the clicking was merely for effect.

One of the great advantages of being a photographer (with a very small 'p') was that I could convince the girls I was doing *glamour* photography. This would entail the girls coming for studio sessions, which was a lark, to put it mildly. Discretion forbids that I should reveal *all* the details of what we were up to. We maintained we couldn't manage with just one model. We needed a stable to make the business commercially viable. Geoff and I told the girls we would give them photos for their portfolios, which, we convinced them, they would find very valuable in the future. They went topless and we would ask them to bring their sexiest clothes with them too. It was a great way of meeting girls and we encouraged them to bring their friends along too, saying that would prevent them from feeling self-conscious and nervous.

I realised that if we could do this to pick up girls, we could also make a couple of bob too. I knew nothing at all about photography, but I reckoned it couldn't be difficult to pick up some tricks. So, armed with a book on photography from the library, I turned an area of our flat into a make-shift darkroom.

For the first time in my life, I pinned a little 'Photographer' badge to my jacket and set off along the sea front, sauntering along, casually wandering up to holidaymakers and asking, 'Photo?' I can't remember what we charged but I offered a twenty-four-hour turn-around. I told the holidaymakers to be back there the following day and their vanity usually got the better of them. They invariably turned up, bought our snaps, and I made my money. I must admit the pictures weren't great. They were pretty grainy because we didn't have much spare cash to buy developer liquid. We had to keep recycling the developer over and over, which affected the final quality of the prints. But, most importantly, this routine pulled in some funds.

Geoff was still working as a pianist in a show bar, backing up a singer called Jackie Knight, a lovely girl from Blackpool. I stuck to my photography. The money we scraped together between us was just enough to survive and pay the rent. I had discovered that, while Brighton appeared to be very lively, there wasn't really a central gathering point, and you couldn't easily find out what was happening. Whenever I hit a new town, I always headed straight for the art college refectory because, firstly, art colleges always have the prettiest women and, secondly, the people there always have a great social life. The quirky thing about art students is that they have a strange, offbeat manner and I was always attracted to this. These people were originals. At that time, the only way to find out a little bit about what was going on in Brighton was through the *Brighton Evening Argus* newspaper. But I knew that there was a lot more going on in town that you could only ever find out about through the art colleges.

To visit the art colleges, I needed transport and fortunately I noticed a bicycle was locked to a railing up the street from my flat. The padlock was not a very sophisticated one, nothing a paper clip couldn't cope with, and the bike was never there at night, only during the day, so I reckoned it must have belonged to a shift worker. So I would 'borrow' it every day and return it at tea time. I 'borrowed' this bloke's bike every day for a week and he never found out. So, thanks Sleepy Head, whoever you are!

Fully mobile, I cycled round all the various colleges, boarding houses and halls of residence where all the foreign students were staying, and I collected details of all the events that were going on. I had managed to lay my hands on an old Roneo, a very simple carbon-based reproducing machine, and churned out *What's On In Brighton*, half a dozen pages of write-ups on various clubs, record reviews, places to go, telephone numbers and cinema listings. I also managed some very cheeky notices.

I wrote the TV column and another guy called Richard Howell wrote other bits and pieces. We street-sold this pamphlet, which turned out to be a very useful device for gatecrashing venues for free. We'd ring up and say that we were the press and we wanted to write a review. We were also invited to all the cinemas to write up the following week's movies.

The cover price was next to nothing, but my plan was to give it away and that its costs would be covered by advertising. But we had to charge for it because we needed to pay for the paper and I was already living on a pittance. So we did this for a few issues, maybe three or four.

While Richard carried on with the Brighton edition, at about this time, around 1968, I managed to obtain a copy of a magazine called *Time Out* that had just launched in

London. I thought it was brilliant, exactly what I was trying to do in Brighton, and its editorial flavour was similar, so I suspected that the people behind it would be fun and interesting. I rang them up and said I'd like to come up to London and meet them.

The *Time Out* office in Princedale Road, Holland Park, was hidden away in a basement down some wooden stairs. When I arrived, I stopped at the top, and shouted, 'Hi, I'm Jeremy Beadle,' to three people working down below, then threw myself down the stairs. It was one of those silly little tricks I was good at, having developed my diving forward roll back in the days of the youth club pantomime. I could also do it down stairs!

When they'd overcome the shock of my surprise entrance, I soon discovered that *Time Out* operated on a very tight budget. Tony Elliott had set it up on seventy pounds borrowed from his mum. It too was street-sold and we discussed the idea of a *Time Out* for Brighton, but Tony reckoned Brighton was not ready for it yet. I told Tony that I would like to come and work on *Time Out* but he said they didn't have the money. I insisted that money wasn't really my reason for volunteering. I strongly believed in the project and thought it could be a huge success. Tony was working at that time with his girlfriend Stephanie Hughes and his friend John Lever sold the advertising. I pleaded with them to let me join, if only they could pay me the bare minimum. So I went to work for Tony for seven pounds a week, which wasn't much more than I was getting anyway, and ended up collating all the listings information and writing some of the cinema reviews.

As I needed to move back to London, I stayed at my mum's flat. Marji had met a guy called Harry Shaffer, a Jewish tailor from the East End whose company, Shaffer & Gilmore was based in Greek Street in Soho. Harry was a larger-than-life character in every sense of the word. His enormous frame would often give way to belly laughs enjoyed by everyone around him. He was on a perpetual but ineffectual diet and was a kind man – but not someone to play Spoof with! Harry was always good company and a lovely guy. He was very popular.

One day, when I had just returned from one of my trips abroad, Marji had told me that Harry was moving in. When he knocked on the door, I said, 'Ah, you're Harry.' He replied, 'Hello, Jeremy, nice to meet you.' For years later, he would always comment on how I carried his bags in. It obviously meant a great deal to him.

They were finally married on my mum's birthday 9 July 1971, at Caxton Hall in London, and they enjoyed a very happy marriage. They both liked their food. They both loved travelling, too, and they spent many romantic holidays together. Harry brought a great deal of contentment into Marji's life.

One day they went for a drink at the Hogarth Club, in D'Arblay Street in Soho. Marji was flashing her wedding ring, and the owner of the club piped up as a joke, 'It's a lovely ring, Marji, but it's a pity Harry didn't buy you a club instead.' Whereupon the opportunity came up and they bought the Hogarth Club!

It was a small Soho afternoon drinking club, and I was officially named its chairman. Harry ran it with Marji, and she opted for redundancy from her other job at Dyn Metal to take on the club. They bought it with her redundancy money and employed a barmaid called Doris. The Hogarth was on the first floor of our building, above a cinema that showed gay porn films. The second-floor studio was rented by Lovely Verna, a lady of the night. Actually, there were *six* different Vernas! Because the girls were paying rent, they had to keep that room busy all the time to make ends meet, so whoever was there at the time called herself Verna. The true Verna was a very attractive middle-aged woman, who sometimes used to come in and share a drink with us. She was very cultured and genuinely French, unlike all the others. She'd tell great stories, such as the one about a gentleman caller, who visited her faithfully every Thursday. There was no sex involved, she said. All he would do was just sit down and eat a plateful of cream buns. While he was eating up, he would just talk to her. That's all he wanted to do. Talk. Other girls would come into the bar and say, 'Cor blimey, that was a bit rough.' But Verna was always different.

Doris the club barmaid was a wonderful character, who stood about five foot one inch tall. I think the inch was very important to her. Though she was small she had the biggest boobs you've ever seen, and used to literally rest them on the bar. She was always immaculately turned out and was terrific with the customers. Doris maintained this theory about drinking which, to this day, I reckon is absolutely right. Doris said whisky would make men aggressive, rum would make them violent, gin was for depressives, brandy was for suicides, vodka was for dipsos and beer for louts. Over the years, I have observed the accuracy of her observations!

The club succeeded as a business as in those days, pubs had to close for an afternoon session and then reopen in the evening. Our club took its real money in the afternoon, when it was frequented by a crowd of advertising guys. We also had 'known faces' – by that I mean gangsters. I remember one guy who said he had six bullet holes in him. He vowed he would never be taken alive by the police. I also remember Mad Frankie Fraser dropping by. He was famous for pulling people's teeth out with pliers and applying electrodes to his victims.

We had one especially amazing regular – let's call him Barry. Physically he always reminded me of Budgie, the Adam Faith character. Barry worked in Berwick Street market, although his real job was as a thief. Thieves took orders, but Barry was very much a chancer. His simple technique was to follow the postman round Soho. As so many offices in Soho had no lifts, the postman would dump all his mail on the floor inside the door of each building, and Barry would go round with a sack and pick out all the interesting parcels, making a tidy living in the process. He used to follow the postman round for hours on end.

Barry's other great trick was to wear a white jacket and march into various offices, announcing confidently, 'Typewriter repairs.' He'd then walk up to various typewriters. 'Hmmm', he'd say, this one needs to come in for a full repair.' And then he'd just walk out with it. He would always dart into the club at different hours. 'Anybody want a typewriter?' he'd enquire. He eventually started taking orders. 'Do you fancy a new pair of shoes, luv? What size? What colour?'

Jimmy "X", who was a notorious Soho character, also came to the club. His wife was supposedly having a fling with some other guy. When Jimmy found out, he went mad! One day Jimmy was quietly having a drink and another customer came in and, for some reason, started niggling him. I happened to be in the bar and as this guy carried on annoying him I thought, 'No, no, no. Don't!' Jimmy asked the guy to leave him alone, but he wouldn't. Suddenly Jimmy just snapped. He grabbed this guy by the ear and twisted it until it virtually lifted him off the ground. The ear is an extremely sensitive part of your body and his victim screamed in agony. Jimmy shouted, 'I told you to leave me alone! If you don't leave me alone, it won't be your ear that ends up hurting!'

We ran the club for about ten years, and rarely saw any trouble though. It was useful to me because I met so many people who'd drop by for a quiet drink or a game of pool. I met conmen, burglars and thieves, advertising execs, people in television and journalists, and a complete range and mix of others.

It was a very exciting time to be working in the capital. Any city can be exciting if you put yourself about enough, but London was the nucleus of energy, creativity and fun at that time, so I felt no regrets about leaving Brighton. An exciting new opportunity awaited me at *Time Out* and I was turned on by its concept. And I genuinely liked Tony Elliott, a man of the time, and a very caring, thoughtful and kind one at that. We had struck up an instant rapport. *Time Out*'s successful growth and development into such a well recognised name owes everything to Tony. I was thrilled to work on the magazine in its very early years, although little did I know that in December 1990 I would adorn their front cover. The edition carried a survey of 'London's Hated Hundred – everything that's loathsome about life in the capital!' and it showed Jeremy Beadle's head stuck on to the figure of Julius Caesar being stabbed. I have always told Tony that he has the worst taste in people and he always replies, 'Yeah, that's why you're my friend!'.

In those days, *Time Out* was the essential guide for hip Londoners, and one day, I suggested that we launch a northern edition. The inner pages would contain the details of what was going on in Manchester, while the outer pages would contain all reviews of national interest. Tony liked the idea, so I took myself off to Manchester to conduct some initial research. I went round the city, looking at the clubs, registering what was going on, meeting people and making lists of events. It was a foot slog because Manchester had a thriving underground, with many clubs and rock venues, small movie houses and a flourishing subculture. Tony paid me to do this but in the end he decided that Manchester alone wasn't big enough. There just wasn't enough going on there to warrant bringing out a special regional edition of the magazine, so he wanted to expand *Time Out* to cover the north-west region as a whole, including Manchester, Liverpool, Preston and Chester.

I always wanted to centre on Manchester because I maintained that readers in Liverpool would only read us to find events relevant to Liverpool, and didn't want to know what was going on in Manchester or Preston, and vice versa. However, we stuck to the plan for the north-west because we thought it would increase advertising and would lead to more outlets, and we launched the first edition on 25 March 1970, with an initial print run of 10,000 copies.

I loved Liverpool and jumped at the chance to get to know the city. The Liverpool Poets were flourishing at that time – Adrian Henri, Roger McGough, Brian Patten, Adrian Mitchell, and others – and I befriended these guys by going into pubs and listening to them perform. Liverpool is always described as the capital of Ireland. Its individual style is somehow Irish-based. And its native wit is unbeatable. Being a stand-up comic in Liverpool is the hardest job in the world. If you can survive that, you can survive anything, because every line you give a Liverpudlian is a 'feed'. As a breed, they are just hysterical. I love them.

At the time, I was busy as a journalist collating information. *Time Out*'s limited space dictated the editorial policy, which was very simple: we only included items we liked. We reasoned that, rather than be negative and write a damning review, why not find things that we were excited by? One of the things that I always loved about *Time Out* was its positive tone. Everything about it was 'up'. It helped to encourage a generation of people who wouldn't normally receive exposure in national magazines. That infectious enthusiasm came through.

Thanks to *Time Out*, I became acquainted with many artists, performers and theatre groups throughout the country. It was while working for the magazine that I first met the eccentric Viv Stanshall, head of the Bonzo Dog Do-

Da Band, who later tragically burned to death. He wanted to talk through some ideas so I pitched up at his North London house. His garden had dolls' arms, heads and legs sticking out from the garden like flowers, and indoors was full of Victorian bric-à-brac, a museum of what most people would have considered junk but which, displayed in the proper context, was really a treasure trove. He met me at the door wearing an embroidered pill-box hat with a tassel, draped in a velvet smoking jacket and clutching a large glass of neat 100 per cent proof. It was 10.30 in the morning but he was already drunk.

In Liverpool, I also met Ken Campbell and Bob Hoskins. They were in the rep company at the Octagon Theatre in Bolton, which fell within my area. I remember the first time I went to see this amazing, anarchic theatre group, spearheaded by Ken Campbell, who was, for my money, one of *the* great original directors, writers and performers. *The Ken Campbell Road Show* dazzled audiences with a brilliant display of energy, originality and comedy. Bob Hoskins played the clown of the troupe. He was hysterical, such a natural clown. Hoskins, in his mid-twenties then, was very acrobatic and wonderfully fast with brilliant double takes. He had short, Napoleonic hair, and a Chaplinesque freedom of limb that saw him twisting and turning his body in tortuous gestures. The first time I saw Hoskins, I was struck by his great presence. He immediately seemed to be a huge star. The conversations we shared were like games of mental leapfrog and gymnastics, as we flitted from one topic to the next. So exciting. I got drunk with them all on many occasions and we would spend many happy evenings talking and laughing.

Ten bi-weekly issues of *Time Out* in the north-west nearly polished me off. The pace was particularly gruelling for me because I was living in Manchester, while we were printing in Aylesbury and typesetting in Seven Sisters Road in North London. To catch the deadline, I had to drive through the night from Manchester in my battered old Volkswagen. The M6 motorway hadn't fully opened then and I would often have to drive over the Snake Pass at two or three o'clock in the morning, travel down to do all the subbing and text-checking, before beetling back. They were long up-and-down hauls, although the great joy of those trips was that I always picked up hitch-hikers.

The sad truth was that we were struggling to sell the advertising and distribution was proving difficult too. As I suspected, people in Liverpool weren't buying it because they couldn't have cared less what went on in Manchester, and vice versa. So one day Tony finally gave up. 'With the greatest will in the world,' he said, 'I can't afford to finance this operation. We're just not making any money.' So it all went belly up. It was a difficult time. To have the whole set-up pulled from under me was very sad.

But little did I know that, within a week, that old revolving door was to spin round for me once again. And this time, I was to come hurtling out and stumbling into the music world.

5

CHEEKY CHAPPIE AND HAPPY HIPPIE

I had about a week to clear up the *Time Out* office in Kennedy Street, Manchester. One day, just as I was preparing to leave and was sifting through my final paperwork and disconnecting the phone lines, the phone rang. The caller was Alexander Shouvaloff, a man I knew well, who was in charge of the North-West Arts Association, which controlled funding for all the arts activities in the region and raised sponsorship for local arts organisations. He was a very elegant, extremely handsome and charming aristocratic chap, whom I nicknamed Silken Knickers. He became an unlikely ally.

The arts establishment had warmly welcomed *Time Out* in the north-west because we had given publicity to activities that normally didn't earn more than an obscure brief mention in local newspapers. On the phone, Silken Knickers said that he would like to see me. His office was just round the corner in Sackville Street, so I agreed to pop over.

He explained that he had received a call from someone who was setting up an arts festival outside Manchester. They wanted somebody to run it for them and Alexander suggested me because, by this time, my work at *Time Out* had built me up a large number of contacts in the media, radio and television and also around the arts scene.

I found out they had been in touch with the North-West Arts Association so that they could qualify as an arts festival and apply for various grants. I went round to this strange antiques warehouse in Salford and met a man called Peter Harris. I was very suspicious at first. I have always relied on my instincts and my original instinct said, 'Stay away!' There was something untoward about the set-up, something not quite right, but I was convinced to take on the job because he had this beautiful brown cocker spaniel, which he absolutely doted on. His affection for this dog and the big fuss he made of it seemed genuine to me, and he pampered it beyond all measure so I thought that any man who loved his dog that much couldn't be all bad. Mind you, Hitler was the same!

Peter told me of his plans for an arts festival. He admitted that in fact he wanted it to broaden its scope, including a couple of rock bands in the line-up. As our conversation progressed I suggested to him that we needed to turn the event into a rock and roll festival to get more people involved. We wouldn't actually call it a rock and roll festival, I said. We would still call it an arts and music festival, in the hope of qualifying for grants. We drew up a contract and I started work. I began organising, booking and planning, while Peter would be in charge of handling all the money and business aspects. That seemed fine, as far as I was concerned, because I never really thought of myself as much of a businessman. This turned out later to be a grave mistake.

A site had already been booked in Bickershaw, an old mining town near Wigan in Lancashire famous for its colliery and its prison. I went to meet the owner of the festival site, who called himself the Count, although his real identity was somewhat less aristocratic. He was a market trader called Harry Bilkus.

Bilkus had a mop of black, dyed, Afro-like hair and used to wander around the market wearing a cape, hence the name the Count. He owned a large, disused pub in Bickershaw, which backed on to fields that he rented. So we had established our headquarters in the pub, and we booked our venue.

Next, I had to start booking all the bands and gathering together items of promotional literature, roping in the help of various friends. Trevor Hatchet, an old flatmate, designed the promotional literature, such as our letterheads and he did a terrific job. Another friend, Ian McCittrick, was an architecture student, and he drafted the site plans. Mac was busy with the plans, Trevor took charge of promotion and I started work finding stage managers and bands. We all shared a flat together in Rainham Avenue in Manchester and suddenly we were all beavering away.

I had absolutely no experience of staging a rock festival. And I had never even really attended one before. So really, I was a greenhorn, starting from scratch. As the idea of the festival grew, we decided that one day alone wasn't enough to embrace all our ambitions. So we decided to upgrade the event to a three-day festival. Our ambitious plans required us to build a self-contained, walled city, where we could not only hold a huge show with all the electrics, utilities, water and gas required, but which would also be secure enough for us to collect attendance fees properly.

I decided to take on all this responsibility because the opportunity to control a rock festival was just too exciting a challenge to resist. There I was planning what I envisaged to be the English Woodstock. The participants would add up to a phenomenal list. I had to keep the arts side alive, so I began booking theatre groups, which was easy as Britain at that time was alive with break-away theatrical groups. On our bill we had circus acts, high divers who plunged into pools of fire, even an aerobatics display of First World War aeroplanes.

Booking bands was not so easy. I soon found myself becoming immersed in the world of rock and roll and I quickly discovered for myself that it is a world full of bull-shitters. Everybody claims to know everybody else. One guy approached me one day and bullshitted his way into my affections on the promise that he could deliver me various big bands from America. He sounded so convincing that I financed him to fly out to America on our behalf. He kept ringing, promising that he was going to book me Frank Zappa. 'Just hold on a few more days,' he said. Of course, this guy was taking us for a ride – a big bloody freebie. I started getting more and more cheesed off with him. He turned out to be little more than a stoned freak, who later re-enacted Shelley's voyage by sailing off into the Adriatic Sea one day while, I believe, tripping out on some substance or other. Unlike Shelley, however, his body was never found.

In the summer of 1970, preparations for the festival became a nightmare. I had very little sleep, worked seven days a week, and travelled up and down to London constantly booking bands. There were problems juggling the money because people had been bitten in the past by rock festivals and were demanding cash up front. Festivals usually worked on the principle that they all had to lose money. This sounds a contradiction, because you were primarily dealing with cash, you could be caught for Capital Gains Tax. Records of the revenues of rock festivals were rather spurious, working on the principle that most people who put money into the event also took money out, although this was never revealed. So, financially, I was on a never-ending chase.

I had built a massive stage, innovative for its time. It formed a central performance area, with wings on either side that formed mobile stages. The idea was that one band would set up on Stage A, which would be hydraulically pulled through to the centre stage. The band would perform and while they were doing so, a second band could be setting up on Stage B. At the end of the first set, band A would be pulled off to the side, and magically band B would appear.

These were very grandiose and expensive schemes, and I was forever chasing Peter Harris for cheques, which included my own wages, not a penny of which had come through, although I was contracted to receive a slice of the action.

I found myself becoming increasingly involved with television publicity, particularly as, at the time, we offered many fruitful opportunities for PR. An MP called Jerry Wigan was busy introducing into Parliament the Night Assemblies Bill, which proposed to do away with big rock festivals. As a result of this piece of legislation, I was constantly being called upon to defend them in radio and television studios.

As we neared the start date, our billing became more and more impressive. I was determined to give our festival a West Coast sound. I wanted to book many bands who really couldn't make it. My biggest target was The Grateful Dead, who were at that time the world's greatest acid band and were led by the great Jerry Garcia. I eventually did a deal whereby The Grateful Dead would make their first appearance on their tour of Europe at our festival, and in return we provided eighteen first-class air tickets, plus a whacking great fee. Because The Grateful Dead had agreed to appear, many other bands climbed on board, simply because everybody wanted to appear on the same bill.

By the middle of April 1972, I had an awesome line-up of stars: The Grateful Dead, New Riders of the Purple Sage, Country Joe (who was Country Joe McDonald), Brinsley

Schwarz (who turned into Rumour), America, Captain Beefheart, Stoneground, Pacific Gas and Electric, Cheech and Chong, Sam Apple Pie, Flaming Groovies, The Kinks, Donovan, Incredible String Band, Al Stewart, Linda Lewis and Stockridge (who became The Corgis). I had jazz from Brotherhood of Breath, Wishbone Ash, Mike Westbrook, Maynard Ferguson and Annette Peacock. I had Dr John, Hawkwind, Roy Harper, McKendree Spring, Dion, Memphis Slim, Jonathan Kelly, the Third Ear Band, Tom McMaster, Dave Anderson and Staircase. Not forgetting the circus acts too. Ticket prices were £2.25 and it cost thirty pence for a dormitory tent ticket.

When we started looking for dates for all this, the most critical factor was the weather. This was rainy Lancashire! I'd been informed by Harry Bilkus and Peter Harris, who had contacted some professional weather people they knew, that the weekend we had earmarked for the festival – 5, 6 and 7 May – was traditionally the driest weekend of the year.

A few days later, I became even more worried when I found myself chatting to a guy called Eric Johnson, a professional meteorologist who worked in the Flood Room at the Ministry of Agriculture. He asked me why we had picked those particular dates when they were guaranteed to have rain. An immediate frisson ran down my back and I suffered an involuntary buttock clench (an ancient meteorological term). He showed me all the figures from previous years' rainfall and, indeed, statistically these days in May were the wettest days of the summer.

But we were all set. The show had to go on. Then, however, as luck would have it, we suffered a few minor hiccups. One of these involved some great gaping holes appearing in Lancashire. Around the site, for a hundred years, there had been deep mining and a series of huge holes suddenly opened up in two of our festival fields, just thirty days before the crowds were due to arrive. They were reminiscent of the famous John Lennon lyric 'holes in Lancashire'.

For weeks, the local council helpfully pointed out that there were more than a dozen mineshafts in the immediate vicinity. The first hole was discovered as a local man was walking through the old Abram Colliery Yard, at the end of Bolton House Road. He told the local paper the ground just 'yawned open' and his dog was almost lost. It was a hole thirty yards across and there were fears that it could spread to five times that size, without warning. The Abram Colliery had actually been closed for about forty years but it was still apparently too dangerous and it was impossible to go near the lip of the crater to see the bottom.

I sent in surveyors of my own to take a look and after their inspection, I was able to reassure people, 'This is not subsidence. These are merely the walls of a shaft caving in!' Suddenly a throng of local council officials arrived and insisted we had to call the whole thing off. I strenuously resisted. 'You can't! People have already started arriving.' They had.

The festival was scheduled to run from Friday to Sunday, but about a week beforehand Bickershaw became the target of swarms of what we would today call 'New Age hippies' who began camping all around the area. In total, about fifty thousand people pitched up.

The council claimed we had to cancel as the festival constituted a huge risk. But, on the other hand, there was no way we were going to cancel. Far too much money was involved. So we rapidly collected together old colliery plans of the shafts and tunnels and I managed to convince the council officials that the tunnels were far away from our field. This didn't stop the alarm bells ringing though.

Our festival was growing into such a big event for the north-west that BBC TV had decided to make a documentary about it. The programme was fronted by a local journalist named Austin Mitchell, who later went on to become a very left-wing, aggressive and brilliant Labour MP, as well as a political pundit on Sky Television, where he partnered Norman Tebbit. The Bickershaw documentary was directed by Austin Mitchell's wife Linda McDougall and they scurried around trying to record all the pros and cons and filming the villagers' reactions were to this hippie invasion.

At first, Bickershaw locals were very nervous about the whole affair. They voiced some outrage and a few people tried to stop the event. But we overcame that opposition. I attended various public meetings and calmed the locals down, telling them about the financial benefits, the amount of money that was going to come into the area and how the festival would put Bickershaw on the map. In fact people became quite excited, and even very friendly towards me. I went as far as visiting the local prison to offer to put on one of our acts as a treat for the prisoners. But the authorities refused to allow me to stage it.

Eventually, most of the villagers welcomed the festival. It was probably the most exciting thing that had happened to this small coal-mining area, which was very economically deprived. But, of course, there were still one or two people who whipped up paranoia about the influx of so-called wild, drug-taking, sex-obsessed hippies. They predicted vandalism and burglaries. A small vigilante committee was organised to try and stop our festival. I went to try to talk to them, charm them. Try to show them some of the plusses.

Then, in the middle of this huge financial and diplomatic juggling act, disaster struck! Peter Harris was arrested just three weeks before the festival. To this day, I am not entirely clear why. It was something to do with a previous business venture that had gone wrong, I believe. This really was a potential catastrophe because he had been in charge of paying out the money.

I was left trying to juggle all the money, while everyone started screaming at me. Without the money, this and that band wouldn't appear, without the money, the fences wouldn't go up, and so on. I also had the difficulty of trying to keep a lid on the story. The news had broken and a couple of reporters did find out, but I managed to fend them off by just saying that he had merely 'gone away for a bit'. I do not know whether Peter Harris's spot of bother with the authorities actually came to a trial.

I was left with the huge burden of trying to raise the capital to complete the show and sort out the business side, which was in a complete mess. We had received thousands of ticket applications and cheques were flooding in but I never knew what happened. Peter Harris, who I'd thought had funding, obviously didn't. He was playing a cash waiting game. We managed to involve some bankers from Liverpool, who came aboard with a very tough deal. They wanted to see their money and they wanted first take of any cash that came in.

Just prior to the festival, Austin Mitchell asked me to give him an interview for the TV cameras on the stage. I'd had terrible problems paying for the fences and, as we stood there on stage, a massive field stretched out in front of us with huge gaping gaps in the perimeter fences. The cameras rolled and Austin Mitchell asked me about the rumours that one of the organisers had been arrested and that we didn't have any money left. 'No,' I said, 'everything is going according to plan.' 'Well,' said Austin, 'What about these fences? We are only a couple of days away now and look at all those holes in the fences.' I absolutely bluffed him. 'They're not holes! They are the spaces for our special security gates, which we are not going to erect until the day before the show.' Well, this was absolute nonsense but it worked at the time! 'You don't expect me to put up the high security gates *now*, do you? If the gates are up for too long, then people will find a way around them . . .' And I remember Austin Mitchell just looking at me knowing full well that he was being bullshitted.

Looking back now, I admit that twenty thousand people must have wandered in free, but there was nothing we could do about that. The bands started arriving and it was my job to hotel them, water them and feed them. As for my own accommodation, I was living in the disused pub. I was surviving on less and less sleep, probably no more than an average of three hours a night. I was becoming a complete physical wreck. Hey! Nothing's changed . . .

When you create a monster like this festival, it suddenly takes on a life and impetus of its own. Its own momentum ensured that it was going to go ahead – whatever happened. The plan was for the bands to perform in the morning too, and not just be on stage in the evenings. But then the rain started. It started to bucket down the day before we were due to begin. And it rained. And rained. And rained. It *really* rained. At the same time, the crowds had started arriving and the combination of the two ingredients was mud, mud, mud, and it was not at all glorious.

Our security system was immediately strained. As the bands arrived, members of the crowd started cutting down the fencing. The security staff were in place but, as they say, 'If your mum isn't on the till, you're going to lose!' The guards were obviously selling tickets and passes on their own behalf and pocketing a tidy sum for themselves. In truth, at the end of the day, it was suggested that only about twenty thousand paid to come in.

The press quickly claimed that the festival was already an unmitigated disaster and that people were getting in for nothing. It was raining hard and people were cold and miserable, but the truth was that, despite the weather and conditions, many people had a great time. I know because I have spoken to many of them since.

1. MY MUM MARJI VISITING ME AT MOUNT VERNON, WHERE I WAS
HOSPITALISED FOR EIGHTEEN MONTHS

2. MY DRESS SENSE HASN'T IMPROVED SINCE MY FIRST PHOTOCALL

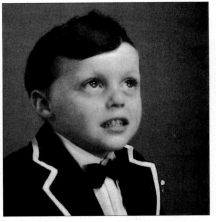

3. (*Left*) MY MUM MARJI REALLY IS
AS LOVELY AS SHE LOOKS

4. (*Above*) PRETENDING TO BE AN
ANGEL – LITTLE DID MY TEACHERS
KNOW WHAT LAY IN STORE...

5. LIFE AT HOME WAS A LOT MORE FUN THAN THIS FAMILY SNAPSHOT
WOULD SEEM TO SUGGEST

6. SIX-YEAR-OLD BEADLE ON MARGATE BEACH, REHEARSING FOR MY FUTURE PANTO ROLES

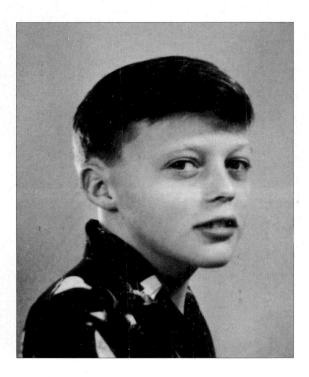

7. AGED TEN. MISCHIEF MAKER? MOI ??

8. MY TRAVELLING BUDDY DEREK DOWSETT AND I, SNAPPED WHILE WORKING AS DISC JOCKEYS IN A HAMBURG NIGHTCLUB

9. FASHION GURU: I TRANSFERRED THE FUR FROM MY SHOULDERS TO MY FACE LATER

10. CHECKING PRINTS WHILE WORKING AS A BEACH PHOTOGRAPHER IN BRIGHTON

11. MY RESPONSE AFTER LBC RADIO GAVE ME THE SACK

12. MY GORGEOUS EXTENDED FAMILY: VANDRA, AUNTIE EVE, CHERILL

13. SEE – JUST A MOUSTACHE
DOESN'T SUIT ME EITHER

14. (*Below*) SELF PORTRAIT OF
THE PISS ARTIST AS A YOUNG
MAN

15. LISTENERS RESPONDED IN THEIR THOUSANDS TO MY 'WRITE TO ME ON WACKY STATIONERY' COMPETITION. PRESENTER THERESE BIRCH AND MY PRODUCER, BAVIN 'BUTCH' COOK, JOIN IN THE FUN – BUT THE ROYAL MAIL AND LBC BOSSES WERE UNAMUSED

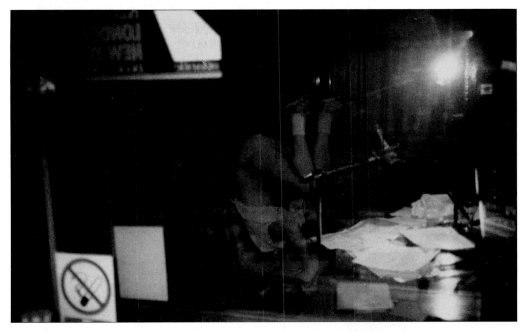

16. LIVING UP TO MY NAME 'BEADLEBUM': I TOLD THEM ON AIR I WAS BROADCASTING UPSIDE DOWN WEARING NO TROUSERS – BUT LBC LISTENERS DIDN'T BELIEVE ME! WELL, HERE'S THE PROOF...

22. MY MOST EMBARRASSING MOMENT. I HAD JUST ANNOUNCED ON LIVE TV HOW MUCH I HATED MY EX-HEADMASTER... THEN HE WALKED IN.

23. MOMENTS AFTER THE LAST SHOT OF *EUREKA*, THE BBC STUDIO CREW EXPRESS THEIR THANKS FOR ALL THE PRANKS I'D PLAYED ON THEM DURING THE RECORDING

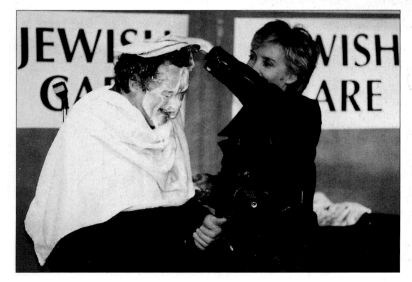

24. JUST DESSERTS FROM MY WIFE SUE

25. THE AFTERMATH OF MY FIRST EVER TV STUNT. THE HUSBAND WAS IN ON THE JOKE. FORTUNATELY THE WIFE WAS GAME FOR A LAUGH.

26. AS WARM-UP MAN ON *MOUTHTRAP*, I DISCOVERED THAT ANGLIA'S TV CAMERAMEN LIKE TO TAPE MORE THAN JUST THE SHOW

27. TONY JO, BEST WARM-UP MAN IN THE BUSINESS, ROMANCES A TEENAGE FAN FROM OUR *YOU'VE BEEN FRAMED* AUDIENCE

Susan Marshall

28. SUE WAS A TOP FASHION MODEL BEFORE WE MET – AND SHE'S LOST
NONE OF HER GLAMOUR

29–32. WATCH OUT! BEADLE'S ABOUT

33. WHEN I AGREED TO RING MASTER GERRY COTTLE'S CIRCUS, THE DEAL WAS SEALED ON CONDITION THAT GERRY DROPPED HIS TROUSERS IN THE RING

34. (*Above*) THE SURPRISE OF MY LIFE – AS SANTA ASPEL ANNOUNCES 'THIS IS YOUR LIFE'

35. AS I EXPLAIN, DIANA'S OPENNESS AND HONESTY SURPRISED ME ON MANY OCCASIONS. SADLY, THIS IS THE LAST TIME WE MET.

36. THE VARIETY CLUB ITV PERSONALITY OF THE YEAR 1995, SURROUNDED BY THE REASONS FOR HIS SUCCESS. (*From left*) : MY MANAGER MICHAEL COHEN, HIS WIFE PATRICIA, AND MY AGENT NIGEL FORSYTH.

37. CASSIE AND BONNIE – WHAT DAD WAS EVER SO LUCKY?

38. IN 1982 – A GREAT YEAR! I BECAME HUSBAND TO SUE AND FATHER TO LEO AND CLARE

39. SUE AND I LOVED VENICE SO MUCH, WE LATER BLESSED OUR FIRST-BORN DAUGHTER CASSIE WITH THE MIDDLE NAME 'VENICE'

40. TELEVISION MAY BE EXCITING – BUT NOT HALF AS MUCH FUN AS JUST BEING WITH THOSE YOU LOVE

Peter Harris only ever paid me three times. I was largely surviving on promises and petty cash. Although many other people made money out of the festival, I was not one of them! When I first started in December, I was paid for four weeks at fifteen pounds a week, two weeks at twenty pounds a week and one week at twenty-five pounds. After that I never received a penny.

To substantially supplement my income, I had signed up with the BBC. I still have the letter from a contracts and finance executive at BBC Manchester dated 5 April 1972, headed 'Bickershaw Festival':

Dear Jeremy Beadle,

I write to confirm our telephone conversation this morning and the arrangements you have made with Linda McDougall to film the activities surrounding the above festival and to conduct interviews with selected persons as required.

We are grateful for your co-operation and, for the facilities you are providing to enable us to carry out this exercise, we should like to offer you a token fee of five pounds, inclusive in this connection, on the understanding that the BBC and its assigns shall be entitled to all rights of television and all forms of exhibition in all countries in the film sequences shot.

Yours sincerely
Maurice S. Taylor.

Five pounds! Not bad, eh?! As you can see, I was rolling in money after that. It was my first ever TV contract. Just five pounds. Not to be sneezed at, you may think, but ironically, *I don't actually think I ever received it.* I think the BBC still owes me five pounds! So, come on, cough up guys. Fair's fair!

My experiences at Bickershaw probably marked the first

time I ever employed some of the skills I had acquired during my travels. I was dealing with bullshitters, conmen, hustlers, shady characters and drug addicts and many of my previous experiences came into play. I knew how to handle much of the nonsense. I knew how to be grateful to those people who were really supportive and, equally, how to avoid those who were merely freeloading. I felt acutely aware of having expanded my role and responsibilities for the first time in my life. Many people and many families were reliant on me keeping this festival going. To my surprise, I actually found myself thriving on the extra responsibility. I became a great optimist, a cheerful chappie, a strange little hippie running this enormous event. I was pretty cheeky with the local council and on television too. As problems arose, I overcame the challenge of tackling them. Suddenly, from being a young tearaway who was considered unemployable, I had become someone employing hundreds of people. Not only that, but when everything looked desperate, I was the one who kept them going and who kept offering encouragement. There were times when I would have cheerfully abandoned things but I knew I'd built up a considerable amount of loyalty among the staff and volunteers. Previously, I'd just been an employee myself. But I was in charge and working for myself for the first time. I realised that I couldn't duck and dive anymore and that the buck now stopped with me. It was time to shoulder some real responsibility.

Each day brought greater risks, tougher decisions and enormous problems. But I embraced them all. I pressed ahead, blindly optimistic and full of confidence that I could manage. I didn't appreciate for one moment the full extent of the project. I have sometimes asked myself, in retrospect, if I would have agreed to take on Bickershaw if I had known up front what I was letting myself in for. And the answer would, without a doubt, be 'Yes!'

I remember fondly the day The Kinks played at the festival and I went into the dressing room of their leader Ray Davis. When I found him, he was an absolute wreck. The Kinks were an enormous band then, but Ray was literally shaking with nerves. I was shocked to see him so jittery. He seemed to be doubting himself but then, of course, he went on stage and performed a brilliant set. The crowds went wild but none of them had seen him as I had.

I also remember Jerry Garcia, the elder statesman of The Grateful Dead, sitting on the back of a truck surrounded by television reporters and radio mikes. I stood anonymously in the crowd listening to him. Someone asked him, 'You say you are a people's band, but don't you think that this festival is just commercial exploitation?' I recall him replying, 'We've only come here for the people and if these greedy bastards make money, well that's not the point of why we are here. We are here to give pleasure to our fans.' I couldn't believe my ears, as my mind raced back to the demands for eighteen first-class return air tickets, an enormous fee and the hotels!

Once the festival began, I did some serious bluffing on matters of security. I personally visited each gate, where I would be given a black bin liner. All the cash was in those bin liners! On quite a few occasions, I strolled calmly through the field, past forty thousand drenched, dope-smoking hippies, while I carried these black bin liners full of cash. I would often stop and talk to people who had no idea I was carrying thousands of pounds in cash in each bin liner. I always wore a smile on my face. I looked like I was just dumping rubbish, but underneath, I was rather anxious. If I tripped up, I thought, or if the bag split, there would have been an absolute riot!

Armed with my bin-liner money bags, I would head back to the pub. Making sure the doors were securely locked behind me, I would dump my bags on the table and empty all the money out. Staff belonging to the Liverpool bankers were there to count it.

The Grateful Dead came in on the Sunday. They were the one act that everyone wanted to see, and they performed a phenomenal five-hour set. I remember seeing an enormous puddle in the middle of the site. Their fans were dancing in the puddle, bizarrely happy. Then, quite suddenly, the rain stopped, the clouds parted and we were all treated to the most magnificent red sunset behind the stage. It was as if our long wait had been rewarded. It was a brilliant moment.

I hardly realised it at the time but Bickershaw was a milestone in British pop history because it was primarily an American West Coast sound. To see all those bands playing together and to have brought them to this odd coal mining district of Lancashire was really quite an achievement.

Shortly afterwards, in 1972 the Foulk Brothers, the promoters who had staged the Isle of Wight Festival, announced they were planning a rock and roll show at Wembley Stadium and they called me in to ask if I would work with them. I was delighted to.

The billing was phenomenal: Chuck Berry, Little Richard, Jerry Lee Lewis, Bo Diddley, Bill Haley and the Comets, Billy Fury, Screaming Lord Sutch, Roy Wood and Wizard. Mick Jagger came along as a guest and was back-stage filming. My job was to fix some of the publicity, so I arranged for Screaming Lord Sutch to present a petition. The Night Assemblies Bill was still active in Parliament so, to attract some publicity, I helped make arrangements for Screaming Lord Sutch to present a petition about the Bill to 10 Downing Street. Now back in those days, Downing Street didn't have security gates so you could wander right up to the front door. Our plan was for Lord Sutch to present the petition to a music-loving Ted Heath along with half a dozen girls dressed in crazy costumes. At the given moment, on a secret signal, the girls all stripped off!

Suddenly there was pandemonium, Screaming Lord Sutch waving the petition in the air and the police, their eyes popping, trying to cover up the naked women. We scooped heaps of publicity for that!

We desperately needed publicity to help ticket sales. So, through various media people we knew, we contacted the TV news programme *Nationwide*, then hosted by Frank Bough. We told them on the Thursday before the Saturday show that Frank Bough must make an announcement that our show was off. It had been cancelled because, we claimed, Wembley had refused to allow the show to go ahead as the hallowed turf had not been covered up and we had been let down by the contractors.

So Frank Bough dutifully made the announcement that the show at Wembley had been cancelled, when in truth there was no problem at all! We just needed publicity. The following morning we rang the studios and said they now had to announce that it was definitely *on* again because, thanks to their *Nationwide* appeal, we had been inundated by offers and scores of volunteers had worked through the night so that the ground was now covered and the show could go ahead.

This way we had two plugs for our money's worth. To be fair, I think the editor of the programme realised they'd been hoaxed but, the following night, Frank Bough was relieved to tell *Nationwide* viewers that the show was now back *on* again and that all the stars would still appear.

On the day of the show itself, I was in charge of hospitality for the artists. I had to ensure the dressing rooms were right, do the meeting and greeting, and guarantee that the stars made it on stage at the right time. Quite a responsibility, as it turned out!

Bo Diddley arrived and straightaway had his trousers stolen from the dressing room by a crazed fan. I was the one who saved Bo's blushes. He was quite a large gentleman, so it was very difficult to find any trousers to fit him, but there was a kaftan available, so I raced round and fetched it for him. He put it on before he went on stage. It looked like a dress but he was very nice about it.

Then Bill Haley turned up with the Comets. Unfortunately I'd put him in part of the dressing room that was previously the men's showers. And they'd flooded! When the he arrived, I introduced myself and immediately had to break the bad news about the showers. Fearing his reaction, I told him apologetically, 'I'm really sorry, Mr. Haley, but we have a problem. Your dressing room has flooded'. I explained that I had to put him with the band in an alternative room, a tiny box area. To my total surprise, he just said smoothly, 'Jeremy, there is no problem. If you could just arrange for the band and I to have some hot drinks and perhaps some sandwiches, then we would be very grateful. And now don't you go worrying yourself about anything else.' He was absolutely charming. This giant of rock and roll, the man who started it all, was so cool.

Then Chuck Berry arrived, clutching a little briefcase. No one came with him at all. His sole travelling companion was his guitar. After my greeting, the first thing he said was, 'Right. Do you have my money?' Slightly surprised, I replied, 'Yes, of course, no problem there.' He pressed on, 'Okay, I wanna see the money.' Luckily, we did actually have the money.

Before he went on he stopped me backstage and, pointing to the mass of fans, said, 'D'you see that girl over there?' A strawberry blonde, very young and wearing a Kiss-me-quick hat, stood out from the crowd. 'I wanna meet her. That is now your job.' So, following orders, I went up to this girl and said, 'Err, Chuck Berry would like to meet you.' This girl and her friends were naturally terribly excited. Later I took them backstage and introduced them to Chuck Berry. Then, I had to leave. When I returned afterwards, they were gone. I don't know what happened. I have no idea, and I don't want to know. Rock and roll attracts its fans and the more devoted female fans are called groupies. The popular image of groupies as very attractive models and beautiful girls who hung around was not at all the case. In my experience, your average groupie was rather sad, a lost soul searching for an identity and hoping that the presence of fame would give her some extra status or position. If one of the bands wanted company, all you needed was a bottle of beer. I'd just go up to the girl and say, 'Would you like to share this drink with so-and-so?' And they'd be delighted.

By the time Little Richard went on stage, we were already running slightly over schedule. He wore a fur coat over this lamé sequinned waistcoat and had hordes of pretty men running around him. He really jazzed the crowd, then got a bit carried away. In the dressing room, Chuck Berry was waiting to perform. But Little Richard didn't want to come off and he started to sing another number, and another. And with each number, he sent the crowd more and more wild. He was out of his head now and just lapping it up. Loving it. Impatient, Chuck Berry was starting to boil. He was livid, absolutely furious, and he was saying, 'What does that motherfucker think he's doing?' His blood was beginning to boil. He said, 'I'm only booked between eleven and twelve and I'm only playing that, boy.' We were trying desperately to lure Little Richard off stage, screaming at him to come off. But he wouldn't. We didn't know whether to pull the plugs, or what.

After much persuasion, at last Little Richard left the stage. And Chuck Berry was waiting there in the other wing. But instead of going straight on, Chuck suddenly turned to me and said, 'I want to see that motherfucker!' I said, 'Look, you're due on right now and we are over-running . . .' That was of no consequence to him. He shouted,

'The reason we are over-runnin', boy, ain't mah fault.'

So then I had to follow orders and take Chuck Berry down to Little Richard's dressing room where we found Little Richard pouring sweat, his make-up all over the place, rocking in a chair, surrounded by his acolytes. As we arrived, he was screaming, 'They loved me, they loved me, they loved me!' Then Chuck Berry walked in, went straight up to him and, pointing his finger said, 'If you *ever* do that to me again, you motherfucker, you're dead! You're dead! I'm the star here.'

But Little Richard was totally out of it and kept repeating, 'They loved me, but they loved me, they loved me.' Chuck Berry replied, 'Wait and see who they love!' Then he stormed out.

Eventually, I somehow managed to wheel the storming, fuming Chuck Berry on stage. While this was all going on in the dressing room, the crowd had been going wild, chanting, 'Where are you, Chuck?' and 'Chuck, Chuck, Chuck.' Eventually the big man went on and started to perform an absolutely outstanding set.

By now the entire concert was badly behind schedule. An official said outright, 'Okay, this artist *must* come off.' Chuck Berry had only done about three or four songs, so we said, 'Come on, he's not even halfway through his act.' But the Wembley man insisted, 'You are only booked to have the stadium for this amount of time and we are going to pull the plug.' So we said, 'If you do that, then you are going to be held responsible for a riot. And there *will* be a riot.' But he insisted. As Chuck Berry progressed through his set, unbeknown to his fans, a flaming row continued backstage. Finally, we said, 'If you pull the plugs, then we are going to make an announcement about what you have done. And we hate to imagine what's going to happen to Wembley Stadium after that. And furthermore, we will not be held responsible.' Thankfully, that saved the day. Chuck Berry completed his incredible performance. The crowd all lit their lighters, thousands of them, and waved them against the Wembley night sky. I'll never forget it.

Around this time I met the legendary Keith Moon. Our paths first crossed when we were both guests discussing the Night Assemblies Bill on a Thames TV talk show hosted by Eamonn Andrews at Teddington Studios. Keith and I began chatting, teamed up and then went out boozing together afterwards. We became very, very good friends. I used to go down to his house in Chertsey and spend weekends with him. Keith role-played the outrageous, insane rock and roller because he enjoyed the attention and the publicity. Much of the time he was completely stoned out of his head and so wasn't entirely responsible for the things he did. But in his calmer, saner moments, which were in fairness rare, he was quite a serious bloke.

Every morning, Keith used to come down to his kitchen, open his cupboard and take out numerous bottles of vitamin pills. So many bottles! Vitamin A, vitamin B, vitamin C, royal jelly . . . He used to cup them all in one hand, cram them into his mouth, reach for a bottle of brandy, take a huge slug and then knock them all back with one huge swig. When the cognac had washed them all down, he'd let out a sigh of satisfaction. 'Ahhhh!' he'd say, 'Jeremy, *that's* the way to keep fit!'

Keith had all sorts of toys, like bikes and cars, but one of his favourites was his hovercraft. It looked like a ten-foot-long go-kart, except that, instead of wheels, it had an air cushion and, behind, a huge four-foot propeller housed in a cage which sucked in air as you fired it up. It was like sitting on a reverse Hoover and was very difficult to manoeuvre. Keith had a huge garden and we used to throw the hovercraft around its perimeter at enormous speeds.

The first few times we went for a spin, I took the helm. If you banged into things, the hovercraft bounced off them and became extremely unstable. We used to create such traps and whizz round as fast as we could. On one occasion, I was trying to beat Keith's record and crashed smack into a tree and was hurtled off the craft. I went flying, even though I was strapped in. Keith thought this was really funny. Then, he said, 'No Jeremy, if you are going to crash it, let me show you how to crash it properly!' and he drove the thing straight into the swimming pool, water flying everywhere.

When Keith wasn't touring, we sometimes went out boozing. Drinking with Keith, no matter how practised you were, was something else. I couldn't keep up. He drank incessantly. And he would never go into a place quietly. You knew when Keith walked in because he had to be the centre of attention from the moment he made his entrance. For a laugh, we once both undressed in a pub and swapped each others' clothes over. I was Keith for the day, and he was me. Keith would be outrageous, a real clown, leaping on tables and grabbing women. He believed in living life centre stage. I was saddened, but not shocked by his death.

Years later, at a charity fundraiser at London's Grosvenor House Hotel in 1986, I returned to the pop business for one night only when I formed what was possibly the world's most amazing supergroup. The event attracted about one thousand people and I was the host. We sold clothes and staged an auction and were raising money for children through the fashion industry.

I knew there were loads of celebrities in the audience, and I was suddenly struck by a stupid moment of inspiration. No one in the audience knew I was going to do this, and I hadn't planned it either. I called out, 'Could I please have Elton John up here?' Elton was sitting with Renata, his wife at that time. Everybody around his table started to panic because Elton is a very creative artist who can be quite temperamental at times. It was touch and go as to whether he would play ball or not. But I knew if I could convince Elton to come up on stage, then I could talk *everybody else* into coming up.

I saw Elton hesitate so I said, 'Don't worry, Elton, you know you can trust me,' which made the audience laugh nervously. But then he joined me, and asked, 'What the hell are you going to do?' I replied, 'Just relax, Elton, no problem.' Then I turned to the audience and continued, 'Now, ladies and gentlemen, now that Elton's up here, I need a few other people please.'

One by one, I called up the stars. Up came Bob Geldof and Paula Yates. No one knew what I was going to do. 'Is he going to slosh them or pie them?' people wondered. Paul Young, Donny Osmond, Jonathan Ross, and Russ Abbot, who had been a brilliant drummer with The Black Abbots before he went solo into comedy.

All these stars joined forces in a unique rendition of 'Stand By Me' and each star in turn sang a verse on their own. Jonathan Ross doesn't have the greatest voice in the world. Considering he was up against some of the world's top rock and roll stars, he was very brave!

Next, I announced, 'Ladies and gentlemen, tonight we have assembled the world's newest and greatest rock band of all time. Here on this very stage. They are also the short-est lived, because they are going to give a one-off perfor-mance. Now, here is your opportunity to go into rock history and also to make a donation to a very worthy cause. You can have this supergroup named after you. It can be named after your son, your daughter, your business, what-ever you like. Their performance tonight is being profes-sionally recorded and you will have a tape of their song. So, ladies and gentlemen, what am I bid for one song from the world's greatest, newest supergroup?' Well, in the end I raised £11,000.

It was ironic that Jeremy Beadle was hosting a fashion

night. Television companies later on spent fortunes trying to make my wardrobe look glamorous. I am the guy who always looks as if I'm dressed in a bin liner. I can't help it. I'm just scruffy. Some people can wear a cheap jumper and a pair of slacks and look like a million dollars. I'm one of those people who can wear a million dollars and end up looking like a bin liner. I can't help it. I probably only ever look in the mirror once a day and that's to clean my teeth.

My brief spell in the music industry was enough. In fact, I ended up hating it. To the outsider, the music world looks glamorous, all sex and drugs and rock and roll. But, in fact, the music business is all about hangers-on, some rather sad women, fakes, frauds and bullshit. I didn't enjoy the people – the seedy business deals, the lies, the nonsense people spouted all day. None of that was for me. I had enough of it all. So I quit.

And then, once again in my life, I was left waiting for another opportunity. Wembley had been a big success financially, but I didn't really have anything else on the horizon. I had met my idols and enjoyed myself to a certain degree, letting my hair down. But I didn't have a clue what I was going to try next. Suddenly, I was left with nothing, no job and very little money.

The next opportunity that was to come my way did so in a very off-beat and surprising way . . .

6

FROM CABBIE TO CURATOR
OF ODDITIES

It was 1972. There I stood, aged twenty-four, living in London, unemployed and virtually penniless. I desperately needed to work to earn a wage of some kind. The phone hadn't rung with offers. No one had been clamouring for my services. Although Wembley had been a success, nothing had turned up. My predicament may sound like a bit of a come-down from the glittering world of show-business but the next great adventure to come my way really was exciting. I became . . . a minicab driver.

I had a very sound knowledge of London because I had always walked around the city. I knew quite a bit of London history and recognised the streets well. I find it almost impossible to become lost and I always find where I'm looking for eventually. I knew North and South London, the City and the West End. I had a car and I needed a job.

When you become a minicab driver, you find out that your colleagues behind the wheel are an amazing assortment of people – out-of-work actors, or people whose businesses have gone to the wall, or ex-criminals who can't find alternative work. All sorts. And you can, believe it or not, earn quite good money if you put in tremendous hours.

The more I worked the more I was paid, so I slogged from eight o'clock in the morning till midnight to build up funds.

Today, I am the taxi driver's nightmare passenger. Having been there and done that I know many of the great tricks of minicabbing. For example, if you didn't know the way, you'd ask the passenger, 'Do you have a preferred route?' or 'Which way would you like me to go?' If people were sick in the back of my car – always a popular event in my book – I'd say, 'You'd better step out and catch some fresh air,' and then drive off. Can you blame me?

I once went to pick up a Nigerian family to take them to the airport. When I arrived I found a husband and wife, four kids and twelve suitcases waiting for me. I took one look at all the baggage and said, 'There's no way I can squeeze you all in. You'll need another car.' But they insisted, 'No, no. We'll manage. Don't worry.' And they tried to load the car up. Eventually, I persuaded them to order another minicab.

When we arrived at the airport, the guy said to me, 'Unload the car and bring my stuff through to the terminal. I'll see you in there,' so the other driver and I obliged. When we'd carted all his luggage inside, he turned round and said, 'Oh, I'm sorry. I've changed all my currency. I have no English money left.' The other driver and I looked at each other in amazement and said to him in unison, 'Well, you'd better go and cash some more then!' But he just replied, 'Sorry. I must go through customs now,' and with that, he called a porter over to load up all his luggage, so I just picked up two of his bags and briskly walked off. This chap came charging after me, protesting. I said, 'I'm putting these two bags back in my car, then I'm coming back to collect the others.' The other driver also took two suitcases.

With all this commotion, a policeman wandered over and, luckily, this officer was very helpful. Once he'd heard my story and the other driver's too, he could see two people were making the same claim. Quick as a flash, the guy pulled out a hefty wadge of cash and paid us in full. Naturally, with all that messing about, we 'topped him up' as well – that's minicabbing jargon for the custom whereby, if you get a difficult customer, you charge them extra, so that a twenty-five-pound fare becomes thirty-five pounds. And with an extra pound for each bag, we made a few bob on that job after all.

I was also given the job of driving an Arab sheikh around for a fortnight. The big deal in those days was to land an Arab customer, because you usually ended up with a Rolex watch or some other gift as a thank you. I had great fun with his car, an enormous left-hand-drive Cadillac. He was staying at the Dorchester Hotel on Park Lane and I drove him around for a few days, then took his wife shopping to Harrods. One day, I sat outside the Dorchester from eight in the morning to nine at night, waiting for the call. Nothing happened. It was incredibly boring. At about seven, I had called up and asked, 'Will you need me this evening?' He just replied, 'I might do. Hold on.' I didn't want to upset him because of that big fat tip at the end of the day. Anyway, at nine he rang down and barked, 'Fetch the car!' so I obliged. He walked out on to the front steps of the Dorchester and ordered, 'Take me to the Playboy Club.' For those of you who aren't old enough to remember it, the Playboy Club was the building *next door*. The very next building. From where he was standing to the front door of the club was all of thirty yards. But he insisted I drive him. Because of the way the car was facing, I knew I would have to drive all the way round the block, so I said, 'The club is only over there.' He said, 'I know where it is,' and jumped in. He just wanted to arrive in the big, flashy car. I pulled away from the hotel, drove all the way round the block and dropped him off. He seemed pleased enough. The doorman at the Playboy Club acted suitably impressed.

Despite the occasional let-down, I was earning decent money minicabbing and part of the job found me, quite often, hanging around in the lobbies of hotels. Browsing around there, I often came across literature advertising the services of London tour guides. Because of Marji and Harry's club in Soho, I knew the West End and all the club owners very well. I knew Peter Langan, and used to go down to Jerry's and Muriel's and The Colony. I had a good grounding in history, I knew all the sights, I was a slick talker and I knew the contemporary scene through my work on *Time Out*. It turned out one could earn fairly good money as a guide. It involved car trips, not only across London but also to Windsor, Buckinghamshire and Berkshire villages, and maybe to Bath, Oxford, Stratford, Cambridge or Canterbury. This all sounded good fun to me, so I went on the course, sailed through it and became a tour guide.

The most interesting aspect of guiding for me was being slightly different. Most of the other guys would want to show off their historical knowledge, whereas I was, you might say, more of a tabloid guide. I knew what the public was *really* interested in – blood, sex and death! So I used to tell the tourists all the scandals, secrets and gossip from previous centuries. I built up quite a fund of anecdotes, and I proved so popular that the other guides started nicking my material.

After a while, I started to design my own routes. I did the best Westminster Abbey tour on the block. One can talk about the building and the structure of the architecture, but I reckoned people are *really* interested in the personalities behind the naves. I would start by saying something like, 'This is the oldest portrait of an English king . . .' then I'd tell them about Richard II, and the various kings' love lives. I would glance up and find that more and more visitors had gathered round me with their guidebooks, having drifted away from the other guides. By the time I was halfway round the Henry VII Chapel, my tour patter would have attracted a huge crowd, and I needed to start yelling to make myself heard. I'd shout, 'and over here, buried upside down, was so-and-so, whose body exploded!' and people would applaud. I invented stories about Dick Turpin sleeping all over the place, I had murders that never occurred, kings who never lived, and bogus English periods of history like the Rubenstein period.

Although I was busy minicabbing and tour-guiding other things were happening to me too. I started firing off a few ideas for television programmes. One of the shows that called back was a Saturday mornings kids' show at LWT called *London Bridge*, starring a very young Pauline Quirk. Today, Pauline's a brilliant actress but in those days she was a great child presenter. I sent the show ideas and went in for meetings. I pitched, they took a careful note of my ideas, and then I heard nothing. Eventually, for my consultancy work I received a cheque for twenty-five pounds.

One of the producers on the programme, Victoria, later went on to work with Russell Harty, who was then quite a respected producer working for LWT. He was hosting a celebrity chat show, called *Russell Harty Plus*, and its producers were looking for ideas. I was one of three contributors asked to come in and pitch. Thanks to my experience at *Time Out* getting me known as this little, furry, friendly freak who used to leap around and turn up all over the place, Russell Harty had already heard of me.

At this time television was hot. I had always regarded radio and TV as exciting media. I liked them because they were ideas machines, but I had no thought of ever presenting or being on screen. I saw myself simply as someone who could volunteer ideas.

I went into LWT and fired off a barrage of different concepts. One was to open their show with a 'Daft Diary,' which would highlight anniversaries of the day with footnotes from the archives. For example, we'd show a bit of film of Princess Margaret marrying Anthony Armstrong Jones. Then we'd freeze the pictures and say, 'But what you *don't* know (and this isn't true but just *for example*) is that he lost the wedding ring that day and what he actually put on her finger was a curtain ring.' We'd show a clip of Roger Bannister breasting the tape and say, 'Well done! The first sub-four-minute mile was achieved by Roger Bannister.' Then we'd freeze the film and say, 'But what you *don't* know is that the man in the background with the stopwatch is Norris McWhirter, who was the timekeeper of the *Guinness Book of Records* and a record breaker himself.'

They loved this idea and asked me to develop it further. I had always been good at quizzes as a kid, and back in 1955 my mother had given me my first *Guinness Book of Records*. I knew the book inside out. I became fascinated by quirky information, and soaked it up.

To develop my ideas further, I started to research the birthdays of various people. I found it quite hard because very little was chronicled about anniversaries. I compiled a dossier and sent off some sample scripts with examples to Russell Harty. And then I heard nothing. Eventually, I rang them and they told me, in retrospect, they didn't think it would work. I was still minicabbing, carrying on with the research, popping into bookshops to look for useful bits and pieces in the evenings, so I didn't mind that much. I was already convinced I'd hit upon a perfect way to index odd information, just by linking all my quirky facts to the day they happened. I thought I could use this format on newspapers, on magazines, on radio and also on TV. So I began to beaver away.

I've kept all my original files. I started with about a dozen reference books on my shelf. Today they have multiplied into probably about twenty thousand books in my reference library at my North London home. They breed like flies! What began in 1973 as a couple of loose-leafed files with the day and the month on the top has swollen now into what must be the world's largest database of dates, events and anniversaries. But more importantly, it isn't just lists of anniversaries. Everything is backed up by strange, odd, weird, offbeat, irreverent, curious information. It's swollen into great big box files, on average two box files per day, divided into eighteen categories, such as birth, death, crime, marriage, animals, science and technology, exploration, entertainment, culture, music, the military ... Now, whenever I glean an odd fact, I'll put a date to it. It may be an event like a battle or a marriage, a disaster or a sporting fixture. Each file represents a day, so if I look up something like the Great Lisbon Earthquake or the Battle of Hastings, there'll be dozens of cross-references to other books. I have about half a million entries in the files.

As I started compiling this database, I realised nobody had ever done this before. I started trying to excite other people. I wanted to pitch it to big companies, such as Shell, and say I'd create them a daft diary of everything to do with petrol or motoring and related subjects. Or go to Nestlé and say I'd do them a diary of everything sweet that happened in history. Companies could then use this information to help with their marketing. I had a meeting at Guinness with Norris McWhirter, who liked the idea and encouraged me to carry on with it. Guinness eventually came back and said that, in fact, while they thought my idea was tremendous, it wasn't for them. So I went back to square one.

Then I met a guy through a friend who was in public relations. One of his clients was a Scottish company called Nairn Flooring, who were looking for a project they could put their name to. They gave me some money to carry on although, in the end, it came to nothing. But it wasn't enough to allow me to stop minicabbing. I still had to fund myself. My working pattern became two weeks mini-cabbing, then a week off for research.

While I was busy collecting all this information I was letting other people know I had this database. I contacted various radio stations, announcing that I was the master of the odd fact, and that my data was catalogued by anniversary. Slowly, the word began to spread. One of the first calls I received was from the afternoon radio show hosted by Jack de Manio, one of the original hosts of the morning *Today* programme. It was a light-hearted magazine programme in those days – today it's much more politically weighted – and it was broadcast on the BBC Home Service. Jack de Manio was quite a character who was also very fond of the drink, but he was very popular with the public and was given his own afternoon show.

I wrote to him and told him I had collated all this quirky material. I ended up going in once a week, armed to the teeth with all my information representing the week's curiosities, to sit down opposite this great man. 'On Monday we shall be celebrating the sandwich because on this day the Earl of Sandwich was born,' said I. And I would proceed to tell the story of the invention of the sandwich. Or else I would focus on the first telephone message, and I'd tell some funny stories about phones.

I also wrote to Kenny Everett, the genius DJ then at Capital Radio. I used to supply him with little facts and quips, writing out the anniversary and adding a jokey tag so that he could compile jingles based around the material.

I soon began also supplying the commercial radio network. I started giving ten or twelve radio stations a list of these anniversaries. I think I was paid the princely sum of about five pounds per list per station. My hope was that eventually every station would take it, and then the Americans would join in and the money would mount up. But I kept on minicabbing.

Then one day I had an idea. 'Why not make this into a cartoon strip?' All the information was light-hearted, zany, offbeat, the stuff I really love, the odd facts you use when you go into the pub. I thought they'd be perfect for a daily strip cartoon. Ed Victor had become my new agent. He is the world's top literary agent, bar none, and Ed Victor, who has today become the world's top literary agent, had just started up his own agency when he took me on. Our first meeting was held sitting on orange boxes in his empty Soho Square offices. Ed arranged for me to meet Derek Jameson, who was then editor of the *Daily Express* and is one of the legends and real characters of Fleet Street.

I remember knocking on his office door and him shouting, 'Come in, Jel!' I had long hair, I'd gone in wearing jeans and a silly jacket, and understandably he treated me like his pet hippie. He said, 'Hey, Jel, let's have a bit of floor shall we?' And with that, we seated ourselves on the floor in the editor's office of the *Daily Express*. When meeting and talking to Jameson, you mustn't be put off by the rough-trade voice. Because he has a barrow boy's voice, I think many people failed to take him seriously, but it disguises the piercing brain of popular journalism. He had a fabulous eye for what the readers enjoyed. Just because a person doesn't have a pukka public school accent, it doesn't mean to say that they don't have a blue chip brain.

Jameson put me together with a great cartoonist named Ken Taylor, and we ended up appearing in the *Daily Express* every day. The strip was called *Jeremy Beadle's Today's The Day* and ran for two years. Within the space of each cartoon, I had to squeeze in thirty-two words, a title, the anniversary and the oddity and it turned out to be a run-away success. Up and down the country, all the drive-time DJs on the radio used to read them out on the air.

One day, a friend of mine called Dave Arthur, the husband of TV presenter Toni Arthur, of kids' TV show *Playaway* fame, told me about an advert he'd seen in *The Times*, which said something like: '*Listomaniacs Wanted –*

*Are you interested in the odd and the curious? If so, we'd love
to hear from you.'*

I sent off a letter to the box number, throwing in a few
unusual lists from history. A Xerox-ed reply told me the sort
of thing the compilers were looking for. 'Nine Breeds of
Dog that Bite the Most.' 'A List of People Who Never Were,
Yet Live Today', such as Superman and Sherlock Holmes.
'Twenty Celebrities Who've Been Psychoanalysed.' 'Twelve
People Who Disappeared and Were Never Found.'
'Famous Left-handed People.' 'Fifteen Renowned Red-
heads' . . . So I sent off my own list with things like 'Twenty
Great Events that Happened in the Bathtub' and 'People
Who Died on the Toilet' (a great, long, strange list).

A little while later, I had a phone call from a woman
called Ros Toland, who said, 'We received your letter, loved
it and would like you to do some lists for us.' I was thrilled
and then I asked, 'Has this anything to do with Irving
Wallace?' Irving Wallace was the fifth biggest-selling author
in history, and had always been one of my favourite writers.
Everybody knew his novels, *The Chapman Report*, *The 'R'
Document*, *The Word*, *The Man*, enormous, million-selling,
brilliant thrillers, but Irving was also a fabulous biographer,
who'd always championed the underdog, the maverick, the
eccentric. A couple of my favourite books were *The Square
Pegs*, which had chapters on different great eccentrics in
history, and *The Fabulous Originals*, which featured real-life
personalities who had inspired fictional characters.

To my question, Ros Toland replied, 'Why do you ask?' I
said, 'Well, it has his thumbprint on it somehow.' She
sounded surprised; 'I don't know *how* you know but, yes, it
is.' I was so excited. Suddenly I felt I was but a handshake
away from one of my great heroes – and by complete fluke.
She gave me Irving's number and I spoke to him and his son
David Wallechinsky on the phone.

David and I are contemporaries. He was so wonderful to

me when we first spoke. He said, 'You are one of us. We have received thousands of replies but yours were the most outstanding.' He said that despite the fact that he was in Los Angeles, he felt that I was one of the family.

So I started work on those lists. 'People Who Died During Sex.' 'Sexual Curiosities about Nine Well-known Women.' 'The Sexual Aberrations and Peculiarities of Twenty Well-known Men.' 'Six of the Most Expensive Women in History.' 'Remains To Be Seen – Fourteen Preserved Anatomical Parts of Renowned People.' 'Seven Men who were Full or Part-time Virgins.' Because I had always been collecting such strange but true information, I needed to organize material into lists, which was great fun as I also added the oddity element.

I have always had this peculiar brain that's been able to sieve away all the important things and only keep the trivial, so it was amazing to become the European editor of oddities and curiosities for their series of books, each one of which sold over a million: *The People's Almanacs, 1, 2* and *3, The Books of Lists, 1, 2* and *3* and *The Intimate Sex Lives of the Famous*. Suddenly, not only was I working with one of America's most prolific authors and his son David and daughter Amy, on all these books, but I was also working for one of my great heroes. Irving would ring me up in the middle of the night and say, 'We need a list, quick.' And I'd say, 'Great! Let's do Famous Noses.' He'd say, 'Okay.' And we'd play this Trivial Tennis over the telephone.

Finally, in 1972, my agent Ed clinched a deal with publishers W. H. Allen in the UK and Bantam in the United States for me to work on separate editions of *Today's The Day* in book format. They took me seven years to compile and write, after which they became massive non-sellers, although to this day I still receive, on average, three or four letters a month from people asking where they can obtain copies.

107

I did receive quite a healthy advance of about £10,000. I had always promised myself that, if ever I made any money, the first thing I would do would be to buy my mum a house. So that's just what I did. I bought Marji a cottage in East Sussex, a ramshackle terraced house built at the end of the fifteenth century in beautiful Ticehurst.

I loved to spend the little time left for relaxing after all these labours watching one of my all-time favourite TV shows, *Celebrity Squares*. One day it occurred to me that, because the programme's questions were based on curious oddities and feeds for gags, my database of information would be perfect for the show.

So I fired off a letter to Bob Monkhouse. I explained who I was and addressed it to Mr Monkhouse personally. I said that I was an 'oddity hunter' and that I felt might be able to help the show. I sent him fifty questions which were obvious feeds for gags and also historically accurate, but I didn't send him the *answers* because I was hoping to intrigue him.

After a little while, I received back a handwritten letter from Mr Monkhouse saying that he really liked the material and that he would love me to come in and meet the producer Paul Stuart Laing. So I went up to ATV studios, then in Borehamwood, in Hertfordshire, and met them along with the writer Dennis Berson, another trivia buff as well as a comedy gag writer. I was employed to write some of the questions, a great thrill and a challenge. The trouble was, I was now doing *Today's The Day* the cartoon strip, *Today's The Day* the book, and writing for *Celebrity Squares*. The work was fun and I was very pleased to be back in television. I would go to the studios to do my writing although, at first, my presence wasn't really required.

From that first day I met Bob Monkhouse, he was delightful. Anyone who has ever met him will tell you how charming he is. Bob Monkhouse has probably given more help at the start of more people's careers in showbusiness than anyone else. He's been enormously generous and influential to many people. It's a great lesson for me to meet such a man, who's been at the top of the business all his life – as a writer, cartoonist, historian, presenter, host. At that first meeting he sat talking to me in flattering terms about how he wanted to know the answers to my questions, and it was a lesson I've never forgotten. How could this Number One celebrity take the time out to help this scruffy urchin off the street? He was absolutely professional. He knew what he wanted but he was always very thoughtful about it. The answers I gave him were as funny as the questions.

When it came to warm-ups on the show, they would need to check voice levels. Bob would say to Diana Dors, 'Diana, how would you feel if you had Theakston's Old Peculiar in your hand?' That's a feed for a gag. As you may know, if you enjoy a refreshment now and again as I do, Theakston's Old Peculiar is a famous beer. As the celebrities would be briefed on the questions, but they would *not* be told the answers, Diana Dors's reply might be, 'I'm not sure how I would feel but I know I'd have a smile on my face,' which would raise a laugh. Then she would say, and this was still only in the warm-up, 'Ah, well, I'd probably be feeling a bit thirsty, because it's a drink.' And then it would be up to the contestant to decide if she was right or wrong.

One of my favourite recollections was of the day Arthur Mullard fell asleep on the set. We were running through the sound checks. It was fairly hot and suddenly this huge grunting noise began. We thought it was a technical hitch at first, until we realised Arthur Mullard was snoring his head off. Under the heat of the lights, he had fallen asleep on the set in front of the audience.

Bob was brilliant. He started talking to him and said things like, 'Well, Arthur, you're obviously really enjoying yourself. (*Snoring noise.*) The excitement is clearly burning you up. (*Snoring noise.*) . . .' Then he started to ask him a

109

string of questions, the answers to which sounded like snoring. 'So what does a pig sound like?' Answer: snoring noise. 'Very good, Arthur!' said Bob. 'And now we'd like you please to do an impression of an old garden gate.' Answer: snoring noise. 'Very good, Arthur, you're really very talented at these impressions.' Dear old Arthur was still asleep. 'What about a low, haunting wind through the night?' asked Bob. Answer: snoring noise. 'Very good!' By now, of course, the audience were wetting themselves and roaring with laughter. Mullard was still snoring his head off, completely oblivious.

Watching Monkhouse at work was a real education. For years on TV he was the victim, the man they disliked, branded smarmy, too good to be true, insincere. I insist that he is *the* most sincere, charming and generous performer. There are certain people in show business whom I call 'palm jobs', whom you supposedly don't like because of their TV persona. But after five minutes in their presence they will have you eating out of the palm of their hands – 'palm jobs'. No one who has ever seen or met Monkhouse will come away and say anything other than 'What a genuinely charming and terrific guy.'

Bob said to me one day, 'You have great ideas, Jeremy, and great potential. You must keep battling. You definitely have something special and you must pursue it. If I can help you in any way, I will be delighted to do so.' I never forgot his kindness.

By this time, I was just about earning enough from all these bits and pieces to stop minicabbing and live off my typewriter. It was a really exciting time. I have always worked hard in my life, but this marked quite a transformation, given that I was once that young dodger who was always skiving off. Now, I was sometimes working twenty hours a day.

I had a business card printed with my name and my new

title, which had been given to me by Michael Aspel, who was then hosting a show on London's Capital Radio. I used to contribute to his programme with a slot called *Beadle's Bookshelf*. I was fascinated by so many new books that weren't reviewed in the mainstream press but still appealed to the mass public. Michael dubbed me 'Curator of Oddities', and I felt highly flattered by that, so I had a card printed with about half a dozen oddities on it. I have always felt very proud of that title given to me by Michael Aspel.

So here I was, meeting famous people, working against deadlines, trying to pump out material. When people ask me to what I attribute my success, I reply that I always drank in the right bars. That may sound facetious but it's not meant to be. It's not *what* you know, it's *who* you know. I owe what little success I've had to picking the right people to work with and having the freedom to choose.

When *Today's The Day: The Chronicle of the Curious* was first published in 1979, I gave it a specially worded dedication to my mother:

'With love for Marji, who sacrificed so much to give her different drummer the space to play. And to Harry for making Marji so happy.'

My favourite poem is 'The Different Drummer', by the American Henry David Thoreau, and it turned out to be Irving Wallace's favourite poem too. My mum made an embroidery of the poem. I was so thrilled when she gave it to me. It's the loveliest gift that Marji has ever made me, and it reads:

If a man does not keep pace with his companions, perhaps it's because he hears a different drummer. Let him step to the music he hears, however measured or far away.

111

Inspired and fired up by this quotation, I often used to work very late into the night. Invariably I would have the radio on, listening to talk radio of any description, normally BBC Radio Four. I was already working very hard as a writer with all the Irving Wallace stuff, the *Express* cartoons and *Celebrity Squares* when I wrote to LBC with what I thought was a wonderful idea. It took them about six months to respond, and I went along to meet LBC's then news editor Keith Belcher and Ron Onions (pronounced On-eye-ons), who was quite a formidable figure. I told them that, in my view, while LBC's prime policy was to deliver news and information, there also ought to be a space for pure enter-tainment and escapism. And I was the man to deliver it.

I explained my idea for quizzes based around the day's events in history, just chatting to callers and having friendly conversations with fun and humour thrown in. The two men sort of muttered and erred and ummed, but eventually they came back to me and asked if I'd like to show them what I could do. That Sunday, I duly trotted in, sat behind the microphone, and off I went. The fee was thirty pounds for three hours. Great money! Looking back now, it's odd that I never realised at the time what a turning point this was to prove in my career.

The show was on Sunday night from ten o'clock until one in the morning. I deliberately wanted that slot because I recognised that late Sunday nights were a bad time for tele-vision, when people tended to turn to radio. Drive time never appealed to me either because it was always packed with too much information – traffic reports, weather reports, news and the occasional records. I didn't fancy that. But, on Sunday nights, I detected a huge, untapped audi-ence out there, waiting to be captured.

Subsequent shows proved I was able to build up a big audience. The programme began very sensibly. I always opened with, 'Hello, sensation seekers!' On air I called myself Jeremy James Anthony Gibson Beadlebum – the reason being that Jeremy James Anthony Gibson was my name – and then I'd say 'and a bum I am.' My show became *The Beadlebum Show*. I threw out all sorts of questions relating to the day. For example, it may have been Anne Boleyn's birthday so I'd ask the question, 'What was odd about the gloves of Anne Boleyn?' Then I'd reveal that she was born with six fingers. The tag would be that she also had three breasts. And I'd throw in all sorts of other related tit-bits, if you'll excuse the pun. Then I'd start talking about the sex life of Henry the Eighth, which was pretty non-existent, although he was quite rampant as a youth. He had positively no sex with at least two or possibly three of his wives. But I digress . . .

Out of the blue, I had a real success on my hands. Fleet Street was kind to me for once. I remember columnist John Blake said I was the only man who made Kenny Everett sound tame. The ratings improved as I became more and more outrageous. I developed an item called 'Beat Beadle', where people were invited to ask me general knowledge questions. If I couldn't answer them, they won a badge with 'I Beat Beadle' on it. Of course, as I was judge and jury for these questions, if somebody asked me one I didn't know the answer to I'd simply say, 'Well, that's a stupid question! Who cares?' And I would make them pay forfeits instead, such as asking people to cover themselves with marmalade while their pet dog licked it off.

On the radio, I attempted items with calculators, asking listeners to fetch their calculators to their radios at home. Then, I would say 'Type in the number 0-7-7-3-4, hold it in front of a mirror, turn it upside down, and what does it read?' The numbers would read a funny word, in this case 'Hello'.

I also started creating crazy competitions. Although LBC was winning great ratings and was pleased with my

113

success, there was a price for being so rebellious. I was always speaking my mind and taking the mickey out of establishment figures. The chairman of LBC at that time was a man named George Ffitch (that's spelled with two Fs). I always referred to him on my show as 'that well-known spelling impediment'. It obviously annoyed him. I never swore on air or used profanity, although I used to use Old English and often told my listeners, 'Go on, tell me something rude.' One evening, George Ffitch collared me in an office corridor, 'You *have* to stop doing this.' I said, 'Stop doing what?' He insisted, 'You can't ask people to say rude things on the radio.' I denied that I was. Rude meant healthy. 'If you are in rude health, then you are in *red* health. I am just asking people to say something healthy to me.' He stomped off in a fury.

I started to build up my repertoire of practical jokes, hoaxes and crazy items. Many people had staged telephone pranks in the past, where you ring up and pretend to be somebody else. Some of the great masters of this are Noel Edmonds and Steve Penk, the current star of prank calls on the radio. But I was more interested in hoaxing *all* the listeners and then revealing the truth at the end of the show.

On one famous occasion, a woman from Willesden called Sheila telephoned. She was put through and I pretended I was the operator, not Jeremy Beadle. I asked, 'Sheila?' She said, 'Yes?' I said, 'Now, we are going to be putting you on air in just a moment. What do you want to discuss?' This was all being transmitted to the listening public. 'What are you going to say? What are you wearing? It may take some time to be put through, so would you like to go and put your stockings on? Go and dress up? People sometimes sound better on air if they do.' She said, 'Now that's a good idea. I'll come back.'

I kept this joke going for three hours. During the show one of her two sons, who were listening at home, left their

114

house, went to a phone box and rang LBC to say that they were in hysterics. I kept Sheila on the line by saying we would be putting her through at any minute. 'Just tell me once again what you plan to say,' I would repeat. We made sure that she couldn't hear the radio, so she didn't know what was going on. People were ringing in all night long and after the show I received sack-loads of letters, just about Sheila. Everyone wanted to talk to her. Somebody even printed T-shirts with 'We love Sheila on LBC' on them. The following week, she came back on and, believe it or not, I played the very same trick on her for about half an hour. By the end, my stomach muscles just couldn't take any more. Luckily Sheila was such a wonderful sport, and she didn't mind.

On another show, I told my audience I had a celebrity in the studio with me and that this was the listeners' opportunity to be an instant comic. We were going to play a new game called Make Stuart Laugh. 'You have to ring in with your jokes and tell them to my guest here. The first person to make Stuart laugh will win a fabulous prize,' I said. 'Stuart is sitting in the chair right here next to me, and is waiting for your calls.'

What the listeners didn't know was that Stuart was my pet spaniel who I'd brought into the studio that night. People were ringing in for three hours trying to make him laugh, telling jokes, singing songs, doing impressions. I said, 'He's looking keen, his tongue's hanging out but no, not a laugh. He's a real wag, I think he's barking mad . . .' I kept coming up with all these awful doggy gags but no one twigged. At the end of the show, I tried to make him bark but he wouldn't. He was only interested in the nibbles I was feeding him. I told the listeners. 'I'm sorry, ladies and gentlemen, nobody has won the £28,000. But I have to reveal that Stuart here is actually related to me. Because Stuart Beadle is, in fact, my dog.'

Thinking about my mailbag one evening, I told the listeners, 'Thanks for all your lovely letters but you're always writing to me on *paper*. This is very unimaginative. Now I'm looking for the most interesting piece of stationery. You can write to me on anything you like and there is a prize for the person who sends me the most interesting letter on the oddest piece of stationery.' Before we knew it, LBC was inundated. We had people writing in on a badger skull (with stamps on it), a whole roll of loo paper, and a complete snake skeleton carrying the message written on its vertebrae. I had people write in on the lining of a fur coat, received one entire message spelt out in stuck-down matches, and was sent another written on the inside of a tin can.

One night, as a throw-away line, I also ran a competition for the person who could send me the most items inside a matchbox. I only thought of it because I had a box of matches in front of me. The next week, LBC tore their hair out handling a flood of matchboxes. The winning one contained about two hundred items – tiny buttons, little gems, match-heads, strands of hair, tiny screws, washers, nuts and bolts, little rings. Marvellous stuff!

LBC asked me to do Saturdays and Sundays, and then suggested Fridays, Saturdays and Sundays. Each programme had to be an event and it was tough keeping up that pace of originality and energy, so I said I only wanted to do the one show. I also asked for more money, insisting I was doing a lot of preparatory work, although most of it was coming off the top of my head live, in fact.

One night, I told the listeners I was travelling around London and I would give them a series of clues. I said I would stop at each location for about ten minutes. If they could catch me there, then they would win a prize.

Live on air, I told the listeners, 'Right, now I have arrived at the Chelsea street where Oscar Wilde lived' (Tite Street).

The truth was that I was actually broadcasting for the whole of the three hours from the usual studio but I was using sound effects of cars, sirens and people talking and walking to give the impression that I was on the move. At one point, I said my car had broken down and I was running to the Underground station. I started panting as if I was running, 'Now, I'm going down the escalator . . . and here comes a train.' Cue sound effects of train. In fact it is technically impossible to broadcast live from the Underground but most of the listeners didn't know that.

I thought this would be a lark and that a few people would join in. But I built up a huge following. At one point, when I said I was at Hyde Park Corner, one of the largest roundabouts in London, a posse of more than two hundred people was trying to find me. I had offered the prize of a track suit to anyone who could find me and they were all after it and me – on skate boards, skooters, cycles, in cars, you name it!

Towards the end of the late-night show, at about 12.40, I said, 'Right, I'm at my last point. I've finally arrived at the home of Doctor Johnson,' which is Gough Square, where the LBC studios are based. I carried on talking. Ten minutes later this enormous traffic cop, wearing yellow fluorescent protective gear appeared outside the studio door. He looked very upset. I could see him through the glass talking to my producer, Bavin.

The policeman was very uptight, so I put on some music and went out to talk to him. He was saying, 'You must stop – now! You are causing a riot. You've created chaos, traffic jams and there are people endangering other people's lives out there, dashing around London. We take a very dim view of this.' I couldn't understand what all the fuss was about.

Then he asked, 'Have you looked outside in the square now, sir?' I replied, 'No, I'm hosting the show, officer. Have you been listening?' I actually wanted to put him on the air.

117

But that suggestion made him even more tense. I told him not to worry, as the show was almost over. 'After we're off the air, let's go and have a cup of tea,' I said. I was trying to be friendly but he wasn't in the least little bit amused.

So I ended my broadcast like this: 'Listen everyone, I must tell you all, if you've been silly enough to fall for all this, that you could have won your track suit by coming straight to the LBC studio in the first place because that's where I've been all the time. This has been one big lark, and hasn't it been fun? Anyway, thanks for listening and see you next week, sensation seekers . . .'

I then left the office and went out into Gough Square, which is pretty small. It was jam-packed! It was just like Christmas Eve at Trafalgar Square. Hundreds and hundreds of people were chanting, 'Beadlebum! Beadle-bum!' They realised they'd been hoaxed but they were still happy! They all had their trannies and Walkmans on and, when they saw me, they let rip this enormous cheer!

When I recovered from the shock, I wondered what we could do with all these people. They would all want track suits! I hurried inside the building again and raided the freebie cupboard. All radio stations are sent free records and books, review copies from record companies and publishers. I grabbed armfuls and, recruiting some help from the phone operators, we handed out freebies. Everyone we spoke to, without exception, said they'd had a fabulous evening. They'd loved the hoax. The only person who did not was the glum-faced traffic cop who, frankly, in his yellow suit, looked just like a miserable slug.

In the end, I'd built up my audience – at a price. The management kept cautioning me, 'If you do this you'll be off the air.' My pranks were sometimes outrageous, but they were terribly tame by today's standards. However they did upset the establishment and, in the end, they did decide to be rid of me. After polite warnings and then sterner warnings, they finally said enough was enough. I wasn't hurt. I didn't take it personally. I knew I was giving the punters what they wanted, but it didn't fit in with the way in which the powers that be saw the station's identity.

I was quite used to being given the sack. I have never been too shocked by that experience. Before I left, I told them I had built them a big audience, and a young one at that. They couldn't throw it away. They needed a replacement who was young and full of energy and ideas. I suggested Tommy Boyd, who originally came to stardom through the children's TV show *Magpie*, and eventually he carried on successfully after I left.

I really enjoyed my time at LBC. I attracted a big fan club among school kids, and I was apparently a cult hero in prisons too! I had fan clubs in Wandsworth and Brixton, and I received some fantastic letters from prisoners. On air I used to say, 'And a warm welcome to people who are in places they don't want to be, like hospital. And if you are in prison tonight, on the count of three, I want you to all shout, "Up yours!"' I'd go, 'One ... two ... three' and apparently, throughout all the prisons within the Greater London area, a whole chorus of voices would yell, 'Up Yours!'

7

A SILK PURSE FROM
A COW'S EAR

My next opportunity came from a young producer called Marcus Plantin who was producing a brand new Terry Wogan game show for the BBC called *You Must Be Joking*. I was thirty years old when, in 1978, Marcus asked me if I wanted to come on board as a writer. We would make films about strange stories, some of which were true, others were complete fiction. Of course, I was very flattered and immediately agreed. I wrote the links and some of the stories.

Terry Wogan was fantastic. We would all be in rehearsal due to record at seven in the evening and Terry would saunter in about five. As the writer, I would anguish and agonise over all the little 'buts', 'ifs', 'ands' and commas in the script. I would brief Terry to say this, that and the other, and he'd read through my script, then mutter, 'Yeah, yeah yeah . . .', before walking into the studio and doing his own thing. In his own inimitable style, it turned out ten times better than whatever I had written. All my gags would go straight out of the window. It was a first-rate lesson for any writer. When you are writing for a genuine star, you must remember the golden rule that stars aren't stars because they are capable of reading an autocue. They have something extra and Wogan has *extra* extra. Terry was absolutely charming and terribly kind with all the crew. People enjoy working with him.

I have always made it a policy not to appear on chat shows and I have accepted invitations from very few. But years later I agreed to do Terry Wogan's chat show, which was pre-recorded. The other guests on the night were the world champion boxer Chris Eubank and Rod Stewart. Terry was very mischievous that evening. Many people think Terry hogs interviews but what they don't realise is that he's actually *saving* an interview much of the time, especially when he has an interviewee who isn't coping very well. He rescues them deftly. He's a wonderful wordsmith.

Terry was talking about Rod's nose at one point, being as delicate as he could on the subject. When he turned to me, I said, 'Well, we've talked about Rod Stewart's nose but what we have here is a genuine and brilliant superstar. We should really be admiring his musical talent, not the size of his nose, Terry!' The audience erupted. They were on my side.

A little later Chris Eubank started up. Now Chris would adopt a pose, which some people think is very arrogant and indeed possibly is. He started on about what it was to be a man. With his wonderful lisp, he said, 'To be a man one has to be virtuous, one must be without vice, one must be totally pure, and to be pure, one must dedicate one's life to achieving greatness following the ideal of good . . .' And he went on and on and on . . . This tirade lasted about eight minutes, and all this time I just sat there, looking at Terry. And Terry was looking at me. And we were both thinking exactly the same thing. 'Edit . . . Edit . . . Edit.' Like a couple of frogs. 'Edit . . . Edit . . .'

At the end of this speech, Terry turned to me and said, 'Jeremy, having heard what Mr Eubank has to say, would you see yourself as a man?' I replied, 'Terry, I am so riddled

with vice, there is no way I could possibly be called a man!'
I thought at any moment Eubank was going to leap up and
biff me on the nose, but thankfully he didn't. Then Terry
turned to me: 'Jeremy, you shouldn't worry because,
although you take a great deal of flak, you will become a
cult figure.' I responded, 'Terry, I'd rather not become
known as the world's greatest spelling mistake!'

After *You Must Be Joking*, I teamed up with an outrageous producer named Clive Doig. He's a zany guy, the sort
of man who has a stamp collection consisting entirely of
nudes on stamps from all around the world.

Clive knew I had a fascination with – and experience of –
practical jokes. I was still writing cartoon strips and Clive
told me that BBC Children's TV wanted to do something for
April Fools' Day. We put our heads together and came up
with a one-hour special, one of the biggest BBC kids' shows
ever. Called *April Fool*, it was hosted by Dave Lee Travis. We
had to produce it on a children's TV show budget, so we
decided to set up a miniature 'rep company' dressed in
period costume, who would walk in and out of various
pranks from history, which we reconstructed in the studio.
With Dave presenting it, the show proved such a success that
the BBC told us they wanted anything further that Clive and
I wanted to do. So in 1979, we said we would write them a
series, which we called *The Deceivers*, a history of forgers,
fakers, conmen and swindlers, using the same format as
April Fool. We originally wrote it for Willie Rushton but, at
the last minute, he pulled out as he had other commitments,
leaving us with a big hole to fill with a new host.

Clive remains, to this day, responsible for what happened
next! He turned to me. 'Do *you* want to front this series?' I
looked at him shocked and replied, 'Clive, I have never done
anything like this before.' But he said, 'You are perfect
because you know the subject inside out, plus you have written it, and you are enthusiastic about it.'

I had already appeared on screen on a couple of shows as a guest, like on Noel Edmond's *Saturday Superstore*, talking briefly about odd facts from history. So anyway, Clive and I discussed it 'at length' – well, at least half a bottle – and then agreed. Thus I was cast as the host of *The Deceivers*, and despite being fronted by Yours Truly, it turned out to be a great success.

It was a six-part series and I vividly remember the day I recorded my very first take as a TV presenter. I did it in one go. I wasn't nervous. I have never been a nervous performer, which actually slightly worried me at first, because fear can keep you on your toes. I am an enthusiast. I suppose I am also a complete extrovert, who's not easily embarrassed, someone who's done quite a few foolish things in public. So perhaps the natural boyhood show-off in me felt quite relaxed about enjoying this new experience of being on screen. One way or another, I wasn't standing on the side-lines anymore.

At the end of the very last show we decided we wanted to include a joke to reveal that I had also been deceiving the viewers. At that time, I was clean-shaven and I suggested that I grow a beard, which we'd have copied. We'd stop recording, I'd go out, shave off the real beard, put on the false one, come back, refilm the link to camera and I'd say, 'Oh, by the way, there's somebody else who's been deceiving you all this time . . .' Then I'd peel off the beard, and that would be the end of the series. And that's how Jeremy Beadle grew the beard that has since become my trademark.

When I finished *The Deceivers*, the BBC asked me to develop another show. I'd always been fascinated by firsts and the origins of things. I had two or three ideas. One, called *Eureka*, was about the origins of everyday objects. Who invented the safety pin? How were Cornflakes created? Who invented the first bicycle? Who brought us the biro? Another idea was *The Illustrated Dictionary*. For both this and *Eureka*, I would bring in a regular cast, as I had on *The Deceivers*, to re-enact the story of word origins and moments in the history of science. And I was also quite keen on a third format called *The Disposers*, based on funny, unusual and quirky stories about famous murders. Of the three ideas, they preferred *Eureka*, so we went into production. *Eureka* was a great hit and immense fun. It ran for five series, from 1982 to 1987, although I only presented the first, because another door of opportunity opened for me.

I was invited up to Manchester as a writer to work on a programme called *Fun Factory*, a live Saturday morning children's show for Granada TV. My favourite moment on *Fun Factory* was undoubtedly a guest appearance by the incomparable Freddie Starr. I had met him many years earlier in a nightclub. We'd sat and talked for a long time. Freddie did the most incredible act and a brilliant impersonation of Elvis Presley.

The day Freddie came on the show, I had to do a piece to camera. Freddie arrived dressed as Tarzan, swinging on screen wearing a leopard-skin loincloth. He caused total havoc in the studio and the prepared script we'd worked on went straight out of the window as Freddie improvised one joke after another. He zapped around the studio, bouncing from wall to wall like a fly on heat, dashing around, creating mayhem. A producer might think he was out of control, but to the viewer it was plain anarchy and very funny.

Freddie had heard that it didn't take much for me to start giggling. Remember, this was a *live* show ... As I was talking *live* to all the little children out there, Freddie sidled up to the side of the camera with a mischievous, wicked look in his eye. I thought he was going to pounce on me. But he didn't. He just thrust his hips forward, then slowly started to undo his trousers, and pulled out his member. He exposed himself, he flashed his mighty manhood at me, and then started waggling it about.

I went into hysterics. I could hardly breathe! But nobody in the control room – none of the directors – knew what was happening. I was killing myself with laughter and I simply couldn't continue. The more I tried to get my lines out, the more Freddie got *his* line out! I completely fell about and, finally, not knowing the reason, the directors cut to one of the other presenters.

Afterwards, the producer came charging down on to the studio floor and demanded to know what was going on. I was still in hysterics. 'What the hell's going on?' he bellowed. Struggling for breath, I tried to explain. 'It's Freddie, it's Freddie.' But, by this time, Freddie had disappeared. The producers gave me a bit of a scolding. They said I should have been more professional and should have been able to continue. I'm sorry – all I could see were the funny bits.

A few years later, I repeated Freddie's trick when I was working down at TVS in the south of England on a pop trivia quiz called *Pop the Question*. One day I went into the news studio to find their weatherman Trevor Baker reading the live weather bulletin. For a lark, I stood beside the camera and dropped my trousers. He battled on and everybody seemed to enjoy it, but later TVS senior executives decided they were not amused. In fact, they were livid. They declared that they thought I was grossly unprofessional and not in the least bit funny. But I'm afraid there was something irresistibly amusing about Trevor reading the weather and trying to keep a poker face while somebody was mooning at him. I only wish I had more to flaunt than Freddie Starr . . .

Around the time I was working on *Fun Factory* at Granada I met and befriended Jeremy Fox, the son of Sir Paul Fox, who was at various times head of the BBC, head of Yorkshire TV and also one of the great TV executive legends of British television. Jeremy had also helped create *The Krypton Factor* and was its line producer. He was a commercial animal, and was understandably irritated by the fact that he wasn't being paid any format fees for *The Krypton Factor*, so he told me he'd decided to set up his own company selling formats. He'd heard of my reputation and he wanted me to join him. Jeremy raised a second mortgage on his house and created a company called Action Time, which aimed to sell American formats to British TV companies. Jeremy left for the United States, putting his whole livelihood at risk, and started making contacts and buying up formats, and when he came back we started developing some of these shows. I helped rewrite the formats, create new ones and hosted pilots which we could sell. If you're selling a programme idea on paper, you are relying on the executive's vision of what that piece of paper can eventually turn out to be. However, if you buy an existing show you can just slot a VHS tape into the player, show off £300,000 of production, and say to the executive, 'We are going to anglicise this product and make it a hit over here.' That technique, combined with Jeremy's undoubted selling skills, helped make Action Time the most successful seller of formats in British television.

At this time, ITV wanted to open up daytime television and it was looking for a game show to start at 9.30 a.m. We won that slot with a show called *Chain Letters*, which had started life as a failed American pilot, which contained one brilliant element. The difference between a game show and a quiz show is very simple: in a game show you stand up. That's all you need to know! *Chain Letters* was a game show and also a simple word game, but it also had an element in there called Tie the Leader, whereby at any time during the show any contestant might get a random chance to level their score with the current leader when they pressed their buzzer to answer. This meant that you always had a horse race. Many game shows on TV are flawed because, if somebody pulls too far ahead, then nobody can catch up, so the audience isn't really taking part in a race as much as observing somebody walk a victory.

We reworked the Tie the Leader element and staged an office presentation, during which we convinced the execs that the show had great possibilities. It was eventually made at Tyne Tees and produced by a terrific young producer called Christine Williams, who hadn't produced a game show before. The first director was a chap called Royston Moyoh, another great TV legend. I know I tend to over-use the word 'legend' but there are only two things in the world tend to rise – cream and bastards – and one has to realise who are the bastards and who are the cream. Royston is an outrageous, riotous character, who's tremendous fun to work with.

During rehearsals I started the show on a podium, then walked across to muck about with the contestants on the other side of the studio. Later however, when we came to record the show, I stayed in position on my podium until about five minutes into the show, when Royston suddenly called a halt to the recording. I couldn't work out what was wrong. He asked, 'Why aren't you going down and playing with the contestants?' I replied, 'If I do that I'm going to start confusing your shots. I never know when I'm going to do it.' Royston sighed, 'Leave the shots to me! What you do is gold. We want that in.' And that's genius. He saw an element in the show that I hadn't observed myself, and realised that my contestant banter formed an essential part of the show's unique personality. So, from then on, I stuck to wandering around. I think I was one of the very first presenters on a British TV game show ever to leave their podium and go and play around with the contestants. *Chain Letters*, which began in 1987, became an enormous success. Within the first four weeks of daytime, ITV beat the BBC hands down in the ratings and *Chain Letters* dominated the viewing figures.

I worked with Jeremy Fox on other shows. We created *Crosswits*, which is still running now with Tom O'Connor. Another one of ours was *Catchphrase*. Many of these shows that we started have since turned into long-running formats. I was particularly proud of *Pop the Question*, which I developed with a friend named Phil Swern in 1985. It was a game of connections, like the card game Concentration, where you call two cards up and try to match them into pairs. We booked celebrity teams, with resident hosts Chris Tarrant on one team and David Hamilton on the other. They matched each other perfectly because they were starkly opposite in many ways. I also had great fun in 1983 producing another show called *Ultraquiz*, which was hosted by my friend Michael Aspel and based on a Japanese format.

My next visit to America changed my whole career. I went with Jeremy Fox to Los Angeles to meet various executives. Action Time was a lucrative enterprise by now and we were meeting a great number of people, who created many hit shows, mainly game shows. In Los Angeles I worked on various entertainment shows and sitcoms as a writer over a number of years.

I always found Los Angeles a very threatening city. I remember I was there the night John Lennon was shot in New York and, like everyone else, I was absolutely stunned. The previous day some guy had walked into a restaurant in Los Angeles and shot dead seven people at random. America, home of the free. The following night I was going to dinner at the home of the widow of the late movie composer Jerry Fielding who was called Camille. I was guest of honour and was looking forward to the evening because the family lived high above Sunset Boulevard in a house perched like an eagle's nest on the side of a cliff that overlooked thirty square miles of Los Angeles. There were only about a dozen or so people there for dinner – a few producers, a few writers, Michael Deeley who produced *The Deer Hunter*, and Jerry's two daughters, Claudia and Elizabeth.

To reach this house, one had to drive along a serpentine road that snaked its way to the very top of an exclusive estate. When all the guests arrived, we all sat outside drinking, then started to go in for dinner. Suddenly I saw somebody at the door. He was about six foot one inch tall, a large Mid Western American overfed blond, in his early twenties, wearing blue denim dungarees, like someone off a chain gang, and a shirt. I thought he was a bit odd-looking but I assumed that he was one of the guests. I said, 'Hi, how are you?' He replied, 'I'm fine,' and we merrily chatted away. Then I said, 'Come in, join us,' and he did so, sitting at the table with the other guests, directly opposite me. I talked away, being jolly and enjoying myself.

Suddenly, I noticed that Camille was looking nervous about this guy and she whispered something to Michael Deeley, who was next to him. Michael turned around and said to him, 'Forgive me, but I don't know who you are,' and the guy replied, 'Oh, I'm here on a mission . . .' at which everybody suddenly stopped talking and just stared at him. Everybody had assumed that he was a friend of *mine* and I had assumed he was a friend of *theirs*. I turned round and said, 'Wha-wha-wellll, what mission is this them?' He looked me straight in the eyes and announced, 'The Devil has sent me.'

This was just after Lennon's death and the restaurant shoot-out and everybody round the table froze. I asked him straight out, 'So, what does the Devil want you to do?' With a wild stare in his eyes, he replied, 'I've come for my bride.'

Believe me, by this time, everybody was *seriously* worried, to put it mildly. I tried to keep him going. 'Who's your bride?" He pointed to Camille's daughter. I said, 'How do you know the Devil has sent you?' 'I have walked through the fires of hell,' he replied. 'I have seen Satan and been licked by the tongues of evil. They have directed me here to find redemption . . .' He continued his rant in a wild, erratic state, growing louder and more excited by the minute. People around the table were very nervous and felt too frightened to move. Then I chipped in, rather foolishly, 'So, what proof do you have of all this?' He said, 'I don't need proof. I have *these!*' At which he brought up both his hands from under the table and thrust them into the breast pockets of his dungarees. Suddenly everything started moving in slow motion. I was utterly convinced that he was going to pull out two guns, but instead of a pair of revolvers, he pulled out two . . . Bibles! Two small Bibles. A great wash of relief drenched me and the others.

He started proclaiming, 'And the Bible said this, and the Bible said that . . .' Meanwhile, Michael Deeley had manoeuvred himself slightly behind this guy's field of vision. He signalled to me to keep talking while he rang the police, so I was left asking this nutcase questions to keep him distracted. After what seemed like an eternity, but was probably about five minutes, I was given a sign that the police were outside. Michael motioned for me to lead him away. I still didn't quite know what to do. I managed to say, 'It's becoming quite stuffy in here. Why don't we go outside on to the patio?' He snapped, 'You're trying to trick me!' I said, 'No, no, no. It's just that it's a bit warm in here. I am very interested in what you're saying. Really I am . . .'

He stood up, and looked at everybody, then slowly edged his way around the table and started walking towards the door. I hoped the police were outside but what was *really* concerning me was how American policemen have a reputation for shooting first and asking questions later – how would they know which one of us was the madman? (People in Britain today may still be wondering!)

I was still talking to him as we moved outside when, suddenly, three enormous, uniformed police marksmen leaped out from behind parked cars in the driveway. They looked like thugs, holding these enormous Magnum guns. The guns were *huge*. They shouted, 'Freeze!' I was already rigid! And this guy stared at me and his eyes lit up. I thought he was going to grab me, but quickly – Thank God! – the policemen jumped on him first. He put up a bit of a struggle but they managed to handcuff him and shove him in the back of their car. It later transpired that he was an Army deserter, who had escaped from a military mental hospital, but the police also later explained that they couldn't press charges because he, quite correctly, had claimed that he had been *invited in*. In fact, he'd been invited by the Devil! As he stated that I had invited him in, the police told us they couldn't prosecute him for trespass. Nor had he actually threatened anybody, they maintained, although his manner was very menacing. In the end, they told me they would drop him on the county line and that he would not return.

I have another slightly happier memory of my time in Los Angeles. I was working as a researcher on a TV chat show hosted by a couple of singers, Tammy and Tennile. One of their guests was the boxing legend Muhammad Ali, who has always been one of my great heroes. He walked into the hospitality suite and was very charming to everyone. Then, as we strode along the corridor towards the studio floor I suddenly felt this fly buzzing around my head. I kept flicking my head, but this fly wouldn't go away. It was really annoying me. I kept brushing my hair aside to get rid it. I was slightly in front of Muhammad Ali, and the producer was also with us, so I tried desperately not to let on to them how I was being irritated by this pesky fly.

Suddenly I heard everybody sniggering, so I turned round just in time to see Muhammad Ali pull his hand away from my hair. He'd been squeezing his very dry fingers together. Now, if you have very dry fingers you can make a rubbing sound, and if you do it behind someone's ear it sounds just like a fly. The great Muhammad Ali was playing a trick on me! Ali said, 'I hear you're a bit of a practical joker, Jeremy! Well, there's one for the autobiography!' I said, 'Thank you very much indeed. What an honour!' And so now, Muhammad, here it is!

Meanwhile, back in England, the BBC had asked me to become involved in a follow-up series to *Eureka*. They were also looking for a new vehicle for Paul Daniels and they wanted something that fitted his persona but wasn't magic. I began work with an in-house BBC producer named Michael Hurll and we came up with a format which involved hidden cameras, tricks on the audience and various games. It was very much a people show. We came up with the title *Gotcha!* and filmed what we thought was a strong pilot. Once again, although I was only the writer, I helped out on the stunts and also took part as an actor. Even though we thought it was a winner, the head of light entertainment, Bill Cotton, disagreed. In fact, he went further. He announced that, as long as he was in charge, the BBC would never transmit a show so 'vulgar'.

Naturally, I was a bit disappointed because I really had hopes that it would work. The pilot was never transmitted, although parts of it appeared in the Noel Edmonds programme *The Late, Late Breakfast Show* a few years later. I had been cheerfully edited out, though my elbow appeared in one scene. Sadly, the rest of me was properly elbowed.

After the pilot, Jeremy and I took ourselves back to America, where I was coming up with ideas for U.S. shows and also buying formats for the U.K. We went to see Michael Hill, one of the most creative producers I have ever met. He changed my whole career with one simple question. 'I am looking for a show where the people are the stars – can you help?' I couldn't believe my ears. 'Well, fancy that!', I replied. 'We have just done one, in England.' I described how the BBC had just turned down *Gotcha!* but he really leaped on the idea: 'This is fantastic!'

We wanted to develop a similar format but we didn't want to copy the BBC pilot, so we bought up the rights to two American shows. One was *Truth or Consequences*, a show which used hidden cameras to play tricks on viewers' friends and relatives. It had been running in the United States since the early 1940s and was created by a man called Ralph Edwards, the great television innovator who came up with shows like *This Is Your Life* and many more. We also bought a programme called *Real People*, which featured stories about – you guessed it – real people.

Then, we created a new format, called it *The People Show*, and when I came back to England, Jeremy Fox presented it to Alan Boyd, who had just moved to London Weekend Television. Alan was previously one of the BBC's most outstanding producers and had been poached by LWT, who wanted him to head up LWT's light enter-tainment department and turn it into a serious competitor for the BBC. Up until that time, the BBC really dominated weekends. Alan immediately liked all our material – a bulky eighty-page document of ideas. He started working on it, flying over Michael Hill and a couple of his producer contacts from America. Together, we all set about shaping this new project into a prime-time Saturday night show.

We twisted and revamped it into what we thought was a rock solid format, but Alan said he didn't really like the title *The People Show*. We anguished over many, many alternatives. We liked the title *Gotcha!* but the BBC had already made a pilot of their own by that name. Then one day, out of the blue, Alan came up with a title which, I promise you, prompted *absolutely everybody* to protest. 'What?!' we all said. 'That'll never work!' I argued that people wouldn't understand what the hell it meant. But, I was only the writer at that time ... Everyone on the team anguished but that didn't stop him. He had thought up that name, and he was sticking to his guns. The show, he insisted, was no longer going to be called *The People Show*. It was going to change its name. That was final.

It was going to be called *Game For A Laugh*.

8

GAME FOR A LAUGH?
I SURE WAS!

Before Alan Boyd had been poached from the BBC, he had produced *The Generation Game*, which had been a mighty success. Now ITV had their fingers crossed that Boyd would bring either Cilla Black or Terry Wogan over from the BBC. These hopes soon floundered. Taking on *Game For A Laugh* meant they would have had to leave the BBC, which would have been a major leap, particularly as they would have been launching a brand new format.

Plan A had Terry Wogan as the main host, with Matthew Kelly as his assistant, along with Sarah Kennedy. Matthew was already well established as a sitcom actor and comedy star. Although Matthew regards himself as a great comedy actor, Matthew's greatest skill is, in my view being Matthew Kelly. He oozes charm and is also a deeply intelligent and very committed man. Sarah's career started in Forces Radio and she also had experience of news reporting on television. The leap to main, prime-time light entertainment marked a major opportunity for her.

But then Terry turned it down. And that left a serious gap in the cast. We continued hunting around for an alternative avuncular figure. Eventually the Olympic runner Adrian

135

Metcalfe, who was involved in sports programmes, suggested that we should check out an Irish war correspondent who had quite a reputation for staying cool in the thick of many serious and dangerous hot spots, while hanging on to his Irish charm. His name was Henry Kelly. We met Henry, who proved to be charming, amusing and funny and we brought him on board. It seems that the Irish make fantastic hosts. They have the charm and the wit.

So now we had three presenters: Henry as the main father figure, and his two sidekicks Matthew and Sarah. They had all agreed to join the show without really knowing much more about the programme format at that early stage, than the fact that they would be working with one of the industry's great producers. We had a terrific creative team, a big budget, and the target of toppling Larry Grayson's and Isla St Clair's reign of supremacy in the ratings with *The Generation Game*!

As we started working on *Game For A Laugh*'s programme ideas, it became patently clear that none of our three presenters were very happy to play practical jokes. In fact, Henry and Sarah didn't want to touch them at all and were more interested in doing people stories. We planned to open with a crazy game and close with a hidden camera stunt. Being part of crazy acts or reporting were the roles that appealed to them most, so we were stuck for who might present the practical jokes. It was Alan who said one day, 'Well, Jeremy, why don't *you* do them yourself?' Here was another occasion when I was called in to be the writer and then offered a presenter's job. Actually Alan Boyd and David Bell disagreed about me – violently – over beards! David said quite categorically, 'You cannot make a light entertainment star out of a man with a beard. Beards don't work.' Alan Boyd took this as a challenge because he could see Matthew Kelly's charm and he recognised that I loved practical jokes. So Boyd stood his ground and offered me the job.

I was very excited at the prospect, not so much at appearing on the show, but more at the chance to stage my own practical jokes on screen. Two American writers I had met in Los Angeles, Bill Paolantonio and Earl Durham, were also working with us. They were tremendously creative and wonderful ideas merchants. I worked extremely well with them.

We had to record a pilot, so we sent Matthew and Sarah out to cover various stories. One of Matthew's very first assignments was to go parachuting with the Red Devils. Because our show was called *Game For A Laugh*, he had to prove that *he* was game for a laugh by going through with a jump himself. Matthew is very camp and outrageous, and the Red Devils absolutely adored him. But when it came to the jump itself, he was terrified. I knew exactly what he was going through because when I wrote the earlier series of *Eureka*, one of the stories covered the history of the parachute. I had trained with the Red Devils myself and I also did the jump. A few weeks afterwards, I heard that one of the guys I'd befriended had been involved in a very serious accident when one of the team's chutes became entangled. I was deeply shocked and his near-fatal accident served as a chilling reminder of how dangerous parachuting can be, even for the professionals.

Finally Matthew went up to about 2000 feet and jumped. He had been miked up and, as he floated down, he started to sing! He landed safely, but when you do a jump like that you can suffer adrenaline poisoning. You become so hyped up and excited that you want to do the jump again immediately. That happened with me but they wouldn't let me try again because I had only been insured for the one jump on *Eureka*. But Matthew charmed his way in and they allowed him to go up for a second jump. And he broke his leg! As they carted him off to hospital, the leader of the Red Devils saw Matthew's naked legs, which were decidedly spindly. 'If I'd realised how thin your legs were,' he told Matthew, 'I don't think I would have allowed this jump to go ahead at all!'

Dear Henry also became the butt of a running gag on *Game For A Laugh* after I took out a pair of scissors and cut off his neck tie on one show. You can imagine Henry's reaction! After that, at various odd moments throughout the series, poor Henry's tie would be cut in half, for no real reason other than to see the look on his face when he realised what was coming.

We had a great time behind the scenes socially on *Game For A Laugh*. Over the years, I have met many charming, affable producers who hide from you the pressures they work under. They tend to keep many of their problems away from the presenter because, as a producer, you don't want to affect your star's performance by telling them too much of the truth. So for example, I might be presenting on the studio floor and the director would be screaming at the floor manager through the headphones. The presenter, of course, couldn't hear their conversation. I might do something wrong and the producer would yell down the line at the floor manager, 'Tell that fucking fat git Beadle to shift his arse to the left and if he doesn't I'm going to come out onto the floor and I'm gonna personally rearrange him!' And the floor manager would sidle up to me, and in a little whisper, say, 'Darling, would you mind moving just slightly to the left?'

One day on the shoot we used a pair of dusty, old moth-eaten, raggedy moose antlers as a prop. Afterwards, we gave them as a memento to Alan Boyd because they were so ridiculous. They were difficult to carry because they were mounted on a plaque, and anyway you certainly wouldn't want to put them on display at home. Despite this they became a running joke. The skill was to try and land these horns on some other poor unsuspecting bastard. When you arrive on location and checked into your hotel, you might suddenly find the horns had got there ahead of you. Members of the crew found them in their luggage on arrival in America. We had American crew working with us and on one occasion, they were asked by customs officials to open their bags at the airport and inside the cases were these sodding moose horns! They crossed the Atlantic twice, and nearly everyone at some time or other found them in the boot of their car, under the hotel bed, in their luggage, at home, in their office. I don't quite know where they are today but I always expect those joke horns to reappear in my garage at any moment.

On *Game For A Laugh* we frequently gave the victim of a prank the chance to have a joke *back* at the expense of whoever had set them up. We once filmed a stunt involving a couple whom we invited to Southend airport. When a pilot left a plane unattended, the husband said to his wife, 'Oh, I'll just sit in the cockpit, shall I, and give it a try?' He duly jumped in and started up. We filmed his wife's reactions as she watched him climb in the plane, taxi away and then take off! She was stunned. After the instructor returned, we gave her a two-way radio so she could talk her husband down. Then, he started doing *aerobatics* and she became very agitated despite him insisting, 'Oh, this is easy!' She was screaming at him to stop. 'Don't do that! Don't be stupid!' He did amazing twists and turns as he dropped out of the sky. She went crazy until he eventually came into land and we revealed to her that it had just been a *Game For A Laugh* joke. We told her that in secret, over a number of weeks, we had trained her husband to fly.

The studio screening of this stunt for our audience was a few weeks away, so we offered the wife an opportunity to have a joke back at her husband's expense. She was delighted to accept. In secret, we taught her to tap dance. Then, come studio day, we showed the aeroplane stunt to

139

our audience and the husband sat there laughing his head off. He was having a good time. Then, when the film was over, I announced our next studio act. 'Right now, ladies and gentlemen, please welcome the Brian Rogers Dancers.' They came on to great applause and started dancing. A little way into the routine, Brian Rogers, the chief dancer, came leaping over to the wife, grabbed her out of her chair and pulled her on to the floor! Whereupon she went into this brilliant tap routine. Her husband's mouth just dropped open with a thud. He couldn't believe what he was seeing.

My all-time favourite twist occurred when we filmed a set-up involving a young man in the Royal Navy. One of the great delights of *Game For A Laugh* was that we were able to pick up the phone and call people like the Navy and ask, 'Can we borrow a battleship?' And the reply would come back, '*Game For A Laugh*? Yes, of course.' It shows how popular the show was back then that we were able to borrow a destroyer!

We arranged for our participants and the ship to go out on a training exercise, which involved a manoeuvre called a Jack's Stay Crossing, where a line is thrown between two vessels cruising through the water at a speed of twenty knots. People are strapped into a horse's harness and are then winched across while the two ships position themselves to sail in parallel lines. In choppy waters, it's a risky move.

This sailor was in charge of pulling people across. We sent a couple of volunteers across the water first, and then little did he know that we were going to send across his mother, who was absolutely lovely, a gorgeous lady. Her son couldn't quite recognise her because we made sure she had her back to him before she set off. He was hoping that his passenger was going to be a pretty woman. When he saw this was an older lady, he muttered under his breath, 'Oh, trust me to get the ugly one!' As she landed on the deck he was still pulling and couldn't see her face at first, but then she turned round and he leaped back in astonishment – as she delivered him ... his underpants. His reaction was spectacular, exactly like an electric shock!

Afterwards, we brought the woman back to the studio and ran the film, which was great fun. I said to her at the end of the item, 'Did you enjoy that?' and even though she was terrified of water and had needed to muster up a great deal of courage, she replied, 'It was the most wonderful day of my life.' We discussed how her son was on manoeuvres in the Far East, and how she wouldn't see him until Christmas, then I turned round and said, 'Well, here's an early Christmas present,' and he walked through the doors. There, again, was a great twist, and a very emotional one too. She wasn't expecting to see him for about a year but thanks to the Royal Navy, who brought him home in secret, it was a memorable reunion.

Reunions make great television and Cilla Black's show *Surprise Surprise* was, in fact, my idea. I still have the original document containing my proposal. When *Game For A Laugh* was nearing its end and I was looking for a new vehicle, I came up with a project that combined the best of *This Is Your Life*, which is all about reunions, the best of *Game For A Laugh*, which used hidden camera stunts, and the best of *Jim'll Fix It*, which makes dreams come true. I put them all together and I called it *Surprise Surprise*. It was considered by LWT and then put in a bottom drawer, and then, while I was away on holiday, I discovered that they had made a pilot with Cilla Black. They did a wonderful job, but to this day, I like to remind Alan that that was my idea.

The Navy was always very good to us and helped produce one of the best reactions *ever* on *Game For A Laugh*. We were contacted by a mother whose son was a very talented Navy boxer. No matter how hard she had tried to dissuade him from boxing, he insisted on continuing because he loved the sport so much. She asked if there was anything we could do about it.

The son went into a ring which we had rigged up with hidden cameras. His mother couldn't bear to watch him, as she hated to see him being punched. Suddenly, halfway through the fight, his mother appeared from nowhere, leaped into the ring, and started beating up the referee! Then, she began setting about the other boxer, who was in on our joke.

This lad froze! His mouth fell open in amazement and his gum shield dropped out! Fantastic! All his mates' reactions were terrific too, as this guy's mum went launching into the ring, swinging her handbag at his opponent and pushing the referee around. The poor lad was desperately protesting, 'Mum, what are you *doing* here?' She came from the North of England and the bout was being staged in Portsmouth so she had travelled some way for her moment of glory in the ring.

In the original *Game For A Laugh* shows, we used a warm-up artist called Bill Martin, who was considered to be the best. But I had met a Northern comic named Tony Jo from Blackpool. Tony had appeared on *The Comedians* and his ability to work an audience was, and still is, fantastic. We have worked together on hundreds of TV and charity shows up and down the country. One running gag involves Tony telling the audience, 'Just keep on applauding and cheering but *don't stop* when Jeremy comes out. He'll get embarrassed, but keep going until I tell you.' Afterwards, to turn the tables on Tony, I sneak up behind him and pull his trousers down. Although it's simple and silly, something in the English psyche guarantees that an audience will find a man with his trousers round his ankles very funny. We have often *both* wound up with our trousers down, thus ensuring that my evening in studio kicks off with the high level of audience respect that I have come to command over the years. My respect for Tony Jo is absolutely genuine. He is today, without any doubt, *the* Number One warm-up artist in the business. In addition, Tony is much in demand as an after dinner speaker and has found fame with one of Britain's top variety acts as a member of The Grumbleweeds.

Game For A Laugh was tremendously successful. We did three series, then Matthew declared he had had enough. He wanted to be taken seriously as a comedy actor and he was frightened that he was being seen purely as a clown, so he decided that he would leave the show. By this time, he and Sarah had developed a very close screen double act, with Sarah playing Miss Prissy and Matthew, in his camp way, being the naughty little boy, so Matthew's departure made Sarah question whether her role would be the same. Furthermore it seemed a problem to define Henry's role in their absence. Everyone wondered how he would continue.

So Matthew, Sarah and Henry left, and the show lost much of its original chemistry and we also lost some of the affection of the public. We had to look around carefully for their replacements. We had a new producer, Brian Wesley, and there was conflict, which caused problems. In fact, *Game For A Laugh*'s decline was because of a combination of factors. It wasn't just the change of team. Brian Wesley's ideas and my philosophy about certain elements of the show were quite different. I would often feel deeply frustrated and was kept slightly at arm's length during many of the creative discussions, which I resented. Certain suggestions didn't strike me as having any impact. I expressed my views quite forcibly at creative meetings, which didn't make me too popular with Brian Wesley. Then came the only time I have ever lost my temper on the studio floor.

We were in rehearsals one day, and I was becoming more and more upset. I was decidedly grumpy as I strode about, saying, 'This isn't going to work. This isn't going to work. It's all wrong.' It wasn't even my routine and in the end, Brian got fed up with me and snapped. 'Look, I'm producing this show, and you aren't . . .'

Although all the crew were around out of sheer frustration, I screamed back at him, 'You are fucking killing the Golden Goose. You are killing this show. You're not listening to the public. You're not treating it right.' I really let rip and then stormed out. I'd had it.

Later, I was called in by executive producer Alan Boyd. Brian was also there. They were very close socially. Alan asked me straight, 'What's going on?' And I replied, 'This is out of order. The show is being killed. The public are losing interest. We are not retaining the initial premise of the show, which is that the people are the stars. And it just isn't working.' Alan remained quite fierce and said I had to say sorry. So I turned round to Brian and said, 'Look, I won't apologise for what I said because I sincerely believe it. But I will apologise for the way that I did it. It was most unprofessional. It was the wrong thing to do in public.'

The series, sadly, did run out of steam. The viewing figures dipped and Brian Wesley moved on . . .

Game For A Laugh proved to be a hole in one, one of those shows that revolutionised a pattern of British television viewing. I think that when the history books come to tell the story of British TV, it will be recognised as a show that changed the public's viewing habits. It helped ITV finally emerge victorious in the weekend ratings battle, out-gunning the BBC in the prized Saturday evening slot.

It was also a great time of personal change for me, because it was at the end of the first series of *Game For A Laugh* that I met my darling Sue. I'd had a number of relationships, all of which were very happy and quite long lasting. I'd never been one for quick flings or numerous girlfriends.

On 21 April 1982, a date I'll always remember, I was

invited to a dinner party at a friend's house. There was a large round table with about sixteen guests. I sat between two very glamorous ladies, one of whom was the actress Susan George. On the opposite side of the table sat an extraordinarily attractive blonde lady, whom I'd smiled at and briefly said hello to before dinner. All through the meal, the only thing I wanted to do was talk to this stunningly attractive blonde with a beautiful smile, whose name turned out to be Sue, but the seating arrangement made it very awkward for me to chat to her.

Suddenly, she stood up and left the room. I followed her out with my eyes, waiting for her to return and when she didn't I casually enquired where she had gone. 'Oh,' said my host, 'she's gone home.' At which point, I despaired because I thought the opportunity of meeting her was rapidly disappearing into the night. I quickly made my excuses, left the party and jumped into my car. I recalled that she'd vaguely mentioned Hampstead and we were in North London, so I sped off into the night, driving at break-neck speed to try and track her down. I went off in one direction and couldn't see her, so I doubled back and drove off another way. Again, nothing. So then I took a completely different route. I was flying. I've always been a fast driver but that night I was really motoring.

As I bombed along one of many alternative routes heading into Hampstead, I saw some red tail-lights about one hundred yards ahead. I sped up and, amazingly, Sue was behind the wheel. So I waved her down, stopped her and said, 'You asked me for my autograph for your children and you forgot to take it.' She laughed and I said, 'Look, just give me your address and phone number and I'll ring them up as a surprise.' She laughed again. I'd heard that she was a divorcee, so I rattled on home and then phoned her up a couple of days later. I asked her, 'Would you like to meet me and I'll give you the autograph in person,' and she said okay.

145

On our first date, as it were, I took her to Whipsnade Zoo, because, I thought, at least there is always something to talk about there and it would give me a chance to get to know her better. Also, it's innocent fun, so if the date proved to be a disaster, at least it would be a pleasant one. We went to a dolphin show and I told Sue I knew the best place to sit. 'Look at all those people. They are all at the wrong end. *This* is the end you want to sit at because you get the best views here.' I did this deliberately and, as I expected, the dolphins came down the pool at one point in the show. They did tremendous leaps into the air, flying back down again and belly-flopping right beside us, creating huge waves. We were absolutely drenched, of course. Sue found it very funny and I'm not sure *everyone* would find it funny. I knew I'd found my soulmate at last.

It later transpired that Sue wasn't actually divorced, but was in the middle of *getting* divorced and was at that time separated. Gradually, over the next few months, I saw more and more of her and when her divorce came through, we started living together. Sue is an ex-model, with stunning looks and a fantastic sense of humour. She is very funny and very bright, hugely artistic and tremendous company.

She had two children from her marriage, Leo who was then aged ten, and Clare, who was eight. When we finally got together, I inherited a wonderful ready-made family in Leo and Clare, although Sue and I were still quite anxious to start having children of our own together. After about eighteen months of me being Sue's gentleman caller, I bought a house and we moved in together and we started trying for a baby. Being a child at heart, I always found it easy to adopt a child's sense of mischief and fun and I always thought I would want children of my own. But I waited a long time to have kids because it was very important to me that whoever I was going to start a family with would be a wonderful mother. But despite vigorous attempts, we were making absolutely no progress. We bonked for Britain, but it was no good. It was very obvious that Sue, already having had two children, was not the problem, so, after many failed attempts, I decided to go and see a specialist.

We went to see a Dr Rice, a great name for a fertility doctor because rice is the Chinese symbol for fertility. He said I needed to take a sperm count to find out whether or not I was infertile. When the other men saw me stride into this fertility clinic, they all looked around and started glancing nervously at each other. They must have thought Jeremy Beadle was secretly filming the place because a few of them immediately leaped up and rushed out to the toilet.

A nurse briskly gave me this tiny little sperm sample tube. Right in front of all these people I found this very embarrassing, of course. I looked at her and said to her, 'Who do you think I am? Robin Hood?' I wasn't sure how accurate I could be at targeting such a small tube! Anyway, as for my quip, not a spark, not a titter! They led me down to this little box room, and there, to 'help me on my way', was a magazine lying on the table. Now, it was immediately obvious that this magazine had been supplied to the clinic by a dyslexic nurse because it was a copy of *Country Life*!

So, I kid you not, to help me get in the mood, I flicked through *Country Life*. Oily Barbour jackets and erect fishing rods were a real turn-on, I can tell you! A while later, I emerged to proudly hand over my specimen to the nurse and about one week later, Dr Rice called us back. The good news was that I was not infertile, which, I must say, was an immense relief. That's why, subsequently, I have always felt enormous sympathy for people who have been in this position. I want to give support to people who go through that anguish. When a public figure talks openly about his experiences in this area, it can benefit many people and give them tremendous encouragement.

Dr Rice told me, 'You're not infertile. In fact, you have a

sperm count of seventeen million . . .' Upon which, my chest puffed out like a bird doing a mating dance. 'But,' he quickly continued, 'to be *actively* fertile, you need to have a minimum sperm count of forty-five million. And to guarantee your chances of success, you need to rate at around eighty million.'

He then asked me, 'What type of underpants do you wear?' I said, 'Y-fronts.' Whereupon, he explained that I needed to switch to boxer shorts. The testicles are on the outside of the body – if you think about it, it is odd that something so vital to reproduction should be placed in such a vulnerable position. Sperm, he said, needs to be three degrees cooler than the rest of the body in order to be active. Men's fashion often dictates tight trousers and tight Y-fronts, which could raise the temperature and burn and kill off their sperm. Then he asked, 'Do you drink?' I coughed politely and replied, 'A little.' He said, 'From now on, no alcohol!' Alcohol is a sperm killer! He continued that he wanted me to wash my bollocks (I *think* that was the word he used) in freezing cold water for about two minutes every morning and every night. Then he demonstrated how this was to be done in a particular way which involved gripping the testicles and pushing them close to the skin of the sack. Then I had to use a cold spray to wash them.

Well, Dear Reader, I have to tell you that this is not exactly my idea of eroticism because the last thing in the world I want to do after I freeze my bollocks off is have sex. But, nonetheless, in the hope of doing some good, I religiously followed this regime for about a month, every morning and every evening. I jetted freezing cold water on my bollocks, I stopped drinking alcohol, and changed from Y-fronts to boxer shorts. Then I went back to the clinic for another test, and after another quick flick through *Country Life*, Dr Rice announced that my sperm count had soared to seventy-two million! Sue and I celebrated by joyously proceeding to bonk for Britain *and the world*. After about six months we were seriously thinking this wasn't going to happen, and were starting to consider alternative methods, when Sue suddenly fell pregnant with Cassie. Many men feel that a low sperm count is synonymous with a low macho count. But, as I now know from personal experience, that's a load of bollocks – freezing bollocks!

Cassie's birth was very traumatic. It was 1 December 1985, and Sue was very close to her due date. I remember waking up that morning to find that the bed sheets were covered in blood. She was haemorrhaging very badly. I knew I didn't have time to ring an ambulance so I helped Sue make herself ready and phoned the hospital to say I was bringing her down in the car straightaway.

The hospital was about twenty minutes away. We were living in Muswell Hill in North London, and the Wellington Hospital was in Swiss Cottage. It was a crisp winter morning, full of bright sunlight. Obviously I was very, very anxious, but I was concerned to look completely calm for Sue. I have always flattered myself that, in real emergencies, I've stayed calm and collected and been able to put things into perspective. Sue was being extremely brave. She didn't panic but was obviously worried beyond measure and I couldn't help but think that, at the very last moment, we might lose the baby we had so longed for.

When we arrived at the hospital, Sue was rushed into theatre and I wanted to be present at the birth. The doctor who'd taken Sue to the operating theatre came out and said, 'I must stress that this is a very delicate time,' and he looked at me. And I looked at him. And I saved him the question. I said 'If there is any doubt about what to do, you must save Sue.' In retrospect, this may sound a little melodramatic but I knew what he was asking me.

I waited anxiously outside on the ward and then, at twenty-seven minutes past ten, just as the sun came blistering through the clouds outside, I heard a baby cry. And the doctor came out and said, 'Both are well.' It was such a fantastic moment. I have always told Cassie that she was born on a sunbeam and she loves that idea.

Another beautiful moment came that afternoon when Sue was in bed with baby Cassie lying beside us. I had secretly contacted our friend David Hamilton, who was working at BBC Radio Two, and had asked him to do me a favour. I turned on the radio near her bed and suggested that Sue listen closely. I'd asked David to play her a dedication, and right on cue, at 4.25 came the message. 'Now,' said David over the radio, 'special congratulations to Sue and Jeremy Beadle who have just been delivered a beautiful baby girl, Cassandra. And here, for the baby, is something that Jeremy has asked for.' It was Joan Baez singing a number Bob Dylan wrote for his baby. It was called 'Stay Forever Young'.

When it came to naming our baby, we'd gone through many different names and finally decided on Cassandra, which could be shortened to Cassie, which we both liked. But we also wanted a middle name. We wanted to bless her with the most beautiful thing we could think of, and so we gave her the middle name of Venice. We didn't choose the name of that beautiful place for the obvious reason that she might have been conceived there – she'd be more likely to have been named Ford Cortina in that case – but Sue and I had spent a long weekend together in Venice and had found it to be the most romantic city in the world. We adored it.

I spent five days in Venice with Sue in 1984 and our visit was unforgettable. We drank at Harry's Bar, one of those exotic places where you sip cocktails. After a while, the owner asked me: 'Well, aren't you going to steal an ashtray? *Everybody* steals an ashtray from Harry's Bar!' Then he led us into the back where his shelves were stacked with hundreds and hundreds of these cheap ashtrays with 'Harry's

Bar' written on them. He explained it is a national sport to nick one of these ashtrays. 'So,' he said, 'will you *please* take one!' I said: 'Well, do you want me to *nick* it or to *take* one as a gift?' He said: 'Oh, for God's sake, just have it!'

The sunsets in Venice are fabulous, extremely romantic. But the most romantic thing I did for Sue in Venice was to fake a heart attack! Yes, that's not a misprint, folks! We stayed at the Hotel Danieli, which is one of the finest in the world. When I picked up the bill on our last day, I treated Sue to my 'death-of-a-fly' routine, in which I bounced around the reception area, crashing against pieces of furniture, falling on the floor, kicking my legs and generally staggering about. I looked at our hotel bill, clutched my chest and pointed to the total as I went down in the lobby. Sue wasn't really prepared for my antics. She just stood there laughing. Anyone who has ever stayed at the Danieli will understand the shock I suffered at that moment, when suddenly commercial reality re-enters your life at the end of a very romantic stay in Venice.

Everyone, at some point in their life, should sing to the one they love and, yes, we went on a gondola and, yes, I did stand up and deliver my *Just One Cornetto* routine. As I began singing, our gondolier rolled his eyeballs heavenward and the other passing gondoliers all shrugged their shoulders. Admittedly, I do have the world's worst voice. When Beadle sings it can be an excruciating experience but I enjoyed myself. Little did I know that I would soon have another reason to sing with joy.

I had resigned myself to the probability that Sue and I would only have the one child because of my low sperm count. But on 14 February, Valentine's Day, 1987, I went into our bathroom to clean my teeth and found a little Valentine's Day box on the mirror shelf. Inside was a pregnancy tester, showing 'positive'. That was my Valentine's Day card for that year!

151

This time I was allowed to be present at the birth. I had never been squeamish before. Sue had a Caesarian and I remember sitting at the top of the operating table, next to Sue's head, devoting much of my energy to making everyone laugh. Sue couldn't feel anything but every time the medical team picked up a surgical instrument, there would be a loud metal 'plang', which I feared might disturb Sue. So, whenever I saw anybody reaching for a clamp or a tong, I would crack a joke or do something funny, just to prompt a laugh and cover the sound of the instruments. I had them laughing in the theatre all the way through.

Our new daughter was quite difficult coming out. They had to tug on her and, when she came out, we thought they had slightly dislocated her hip. There followed an anxious few months because we thought she might be permanently damaged in her leg, but fortunately, that all settled down and she had a temporary clicky hip.

When it came to choosing a name we tried to think of names that would follow the same pattern we had picked for Cassie. Cassie has a double 's' in it, and we settled on Bonnie, which has a double 'n'. Then we came to thinking of a special middle name, which wasn't difficult because of my Valentine's Day surprise. So Bonnie was blessed with the middle name Valentine, and our two daughters are 'C.V.' and 'B.V.', Cassie Venice Beadle and Bonnie Valentine Beadle. I love them both!

You will notice that this book distinctly avoids mentioning my past girlfriends, and this is quite deliberate. I think it would be unfair to name the girls I have shared my heart with in the past, because they have their own lives with other partners now. I have never really been a Jack the Lad anyway. I was never a great nightclubber or a one-night-stand person and I had a number of very close and successful relationships, each of which lasted a long time. I enjoy the company of women, who can in my view, often be far more entertaining and interesting than men. Obviously, being a so-called celebrity does present you with the opportunity to meet girls, but certain women aren't necessarily so much attracted to you as to your celebrity or power. For some women, bedding a celebrity is almost a notch for them and a number of famous names have paid dearly for a brief fling, especially when those girls have gone public. By contrast, in my time, I have enjoyed some very happy relationships with some delightful and remarkable women.

Fortunately, or unfortunately, celebrity came to me relatively late in life. I suppose if I had been younger, I might have been sucked in. But I didn't really hit the screens in a serious way until I was thirty-two, by which time I'd sown a few wild oats and was no longer fooled by the flirting and the party scene. Flirting can be fun but that's all it is. I am no angel and I have never claimed to be one. I have the same weaknesses as most men. But the prospect of a revelatory, sensational piece in the tabloids doesn't appeal. I think most people would understand that.

Sue and I never married, and I have never asked her to marry me. I have taken an awful amount of stick in the press for that, although *The Sun* announced we *were actually* married one day! Friends often ask me why we don't get married and I always reply that I genuinely believe that we *are* already married. What is a marriage, anyway, but two people making a commitment to each other to protect and to love. And I have done that in every way possible other than going through the formality of a marriage ceremony. I suppose I was raised during a time of flowers in your hair and hippies, when the popularity of marriage as an institution had seriously declined. When I realised I was with the person I wanted to share my life with, that was enough.

There seems no reason to go through any ceremony, and I certainly wouldn't want a religious ceremony myself because that would be hypocritical for me. It may sound strange coming from a man who was born illegitimate, as my children could be cast with the same stigma as I was in my youth. But today, single-parent families are commonplace. My own mother's values – a sense of dignity and morality – had a major influence on my attitudes to such issues. Although Marji eventually tied the knot at a register office when she married Harry, she would never put pressure on me. Her concern is for Sue and the children and she knows they are safe and loved. I have probably made more financial arrangements to support my family than many men because, since no legal marriage contract exists between Sue and me, under the tax rules of this country, I have to be extra careful. I have made sure that, in the event of my death, property and monies will go to them. And I have gone to enormous lengths to secure my family's future.

A friend of mine lived very happily with his partner for years. Suddenly they married. Two years later he walked out. He came to me and asked me to hide him as he needed to get away from everybody. I took him for a drink to our local pub and said, 'I am only going to ask you one question and if you don't want to answer it, then don't. But I am intrigued to know *why* you got married?' He turned to me, shrugged and said, 'Jeremy, I forgot to say No.' I can cite instantly one, two, three, half a dozen friends who lived very happily with their partners for a long time, then decided to marry . . . and their relationship fell apart so quickly it was untrue. It is almost predictable and certainly frightening.

There are probably times when Sue feels, for Cassie's and Bonnie's sakes, that it would be nice for us to formalise our marriage. Who knows, maybe one day I shall! There are no absolutes between us on that issue. At the moment, I just don't think that signing a legally binding marriage contract would make any difference at all. I certainly wouldn't walk down the aisle. As glamorous as it might sound, it would be too hypocritical for me because I don't acknowledge any formal religion. But more importantly, I think that Cassie and Bonnie realise that I love them with all my heart. They are my pleasure and my delight and they mean more to me than any success. I am a devoted parent, in the sense that I wake up in the middle of the night worrying about the things that might happen to them, and I fear for their safety sometimes. They know that I am their dad, that I love them and that I'll always be there for them, irrespective of whether or not I go through the ritual of a marriage ceremony. To wind me up about getting married, Sue has once or twice jokingly warned me, 'Watch out, it's leap year!' I'd like to think that Sue feels married to me already but you never know what to expect from a man who has always been full of surprises. I would probably organise it so that Sue thought we were going to *someone else's wedding* and, unbeknown to her, she would end up being the bride. Who knows? Or perhaps, one day, Sue and I might give Cassie and Bonnie a Christmas present and get married after all. I certainly think they would enjoy dressing up!

Despite not being formally married, Sue and I do celebrate an anniversary – 21 April, the date of that dinner party in 1982 when we met. I'll give Sue some flowers or we'll go out for dinner. Unfortunately, because we have so many friends, it is very rare that Sue and I go out on our own. I insist that Sue and I go away on holiday together alone every year and, although we haven't had a honeymoon, because we never married, we have always had babymoons. A babymoon is, I think, really important. After the nine months of pregnancy, which is obviously both an anxious and exhausting time for the mother, comes the actual birth, which is an absolute nightmare. Planning a babymoon is my way of telling Sue that I really appreciate what she went through. Sue and I enjoy our quality time together – and, of course, we don't bring baby along. I rarely go out without her. Most men go to the pub, play golf, enjoy sports. I can't remember the last time I went out on my own socially.

I first got to properly know Leo and Clare, Sue's children by her first marriage, when we shared her flat briefly after her husband died. Her ex-husband, David Silverman was a wealthy, successful dealer in the rag trade but he had a serious drug problem, which had destroyed their marriage. Indeed, on the very day Sue's divorce was finalised, he died of a drug overdose. Although Leo was only ten at the time and Clare eight, and despite the trauma of the divorce and David's death, we got on extremely well. As Leo grew older, he developed into a handsome boy, although he was very small for his age compared to all his mates, who were growing taller. This began to worry him, and he began over-compensating for his height by trying to be different in other ways. This led him to exaggerate and invent things that didn't really happen. Teenagers are a nightmare and Leo was no exception. I get on well with kids until they are about twelve or thirteen, but the teenage years can be difficult. I didn't like being a teenager myself. It's a tough time, when you think you know everything but you haven't any power. You're a rebel but you've no money and no status. I remember Leo laying all that on me once, but I told him, 'My business is bullshit. Don't try and bullshit a bullshitter!'

When he was thirteen, Leo, who was very bright, went to Highgate School in North London, a famous old established boys' public school. He wanted to board and, although I didn't want him to because I worried that he'd be bullied, he pleaded with us and won the argument. He did very well and achieved sufficient O and A levels to clinch a place at Sussex University to read engineering. However, he suddenly discovered that engineering had two major faults: (1) he had to work and (2) there were no women on the course. After switching to philosophy, he packed that in too, and instead took himself off to Disneyland in France, which had just opened, and became a waiter. Leo was always most interested in music and he wanted to pursue a career in the music business. I had quite a few contacts but he never let me open doors for him and courageously did it all himself. He eventually found an opening with X-Cel records and today he is the A and R man for one of the most successful labels in the country. Among others he handles The Prodigy, one of the biggest selling bands in the world.

Leo has grown up to be a wonderful man and Clare is a delight. She is also very independent, very attractive and very artistic, like her mum. She left school with excellent O levels and was offered a place at Oxford to read art history, but as she is an exceptionally talented artist, she took a place at St Martin's School of Art in Long Acre in London instead.

Despite Clare's considerable flair for art and drawing, unfortunately some of her subjects leave a lot to be desired (*above*).

Sue and I have been blessed with a lovely family. When Bonnie was born we had been told she might have to wear callipers when she grew older. We took Bonnie back to the paediatrician every fortnight and he'd move her hip around, then when she was about four months old, the doctors confirmed she wasn't going to have a problem after all. I was thrilled that she was healthy. So with both Bonnie and Cassie, I have known traumas – of being inches away from losing a child and then being inches away from having a child who's disabled. When I visit hospitals on charity work, I frequently meet disabled children and I always think of the agony that parents go through. I was in hospital for two years myself as a child, having many operations on my hand and skin grafts on my legs.

Having been born with a disability myself, I knew that it didn't hamper me in any way. Nature has a wonderful way of compensating, so if you are born with a disability, it can sharpen up your other senses or can make you physically stronger in other parts of the body. I think my disability made me able to cope with people more easily. People would always refer to my 'funny hand'. And I learned quickly how to deal with that by using my wits and sense of humour. One particularly vitriolic critic wrote some really nasty things about me and my hand and I did in fact sue, successfully. It irks me that reporters who have met me for five minutes manage to compose detailed psychological profiles of my personality straightaway. Some have suggested that my love of mischief and practical joking is my way of 'exacting revenge on life for my hand'. Nothing could be sillier or more ignorant.

I am patron of a charity called REACH, which works specifically for children with arm deficiency and who have Poland syndrome like me. They may have no hand or no fingers, and to suggest that they are going to spend the rest of their lives reaping revenge for their disability is absurd.

Such a suggestion tells me more about the person making it than it does anything else.

These children are remarkable. In some cases, they are very severely handicapped but they live life to the full and are very happy children. I receive many letters, always from anxious parents, never from the children, saying, 'My child's been born with Poland syndrome. Can you offer any advice?' I tend to write back telling them they must never hide it because that only attracts attention and that their child must learn to use the arm as much as possible so that the muscles don't wither. But the main thing I emphasise is that it is not the size of your hand that is important, but the size of your heart.

Cassie has grown up to be like her mum, very artistic, very clever, but quite shy. She came out of her shell though recently, when she landed the lead role in her school play. She was absolutely brilliant and stood up there and shone. Bonnie, by contrast, has grown up believing one should live life loudly. Unfortunately, she is a little Beadle. In her, I see all the things that I used to do as a kid. She doesn't do her homework, she feels bored in lessons, she's mischievous and easily distracted.

Both girls have phenomenal memories. One moment in their childhood they will never forget is when their dad co-starred with Sooty! I was offered a guest appearance on *The Sooty Show* and Cassie and Bonnie were so excited that I had to do it. I met Matthew Corbett and Sooty and then, on the set, I turned round to Sooty and said, 'If you squirt water over me, I'm going to break your wrist!' I didn't, of course but I got extra wet instead! For Cassie and Bonnie, it was one of their proudest moments – the day Daddy was soaked by Sooty.

When Cassie was born, Leo would have been about twelve or thirteen, and Clare would have been eleven. Despite their age differences, we lived together extremely happily as a family unit and I have always adored Leo and Clare. Sue and I had been together for about three years before our two daughters came along, so within the space of five action-packed years, I went from being a bachelor boy to a proud father of four.

By the time I was forty I had become a house-owner with a 'wife' and four kids. The interesting thing was that for the first time in my life I had to look seriously at earning a living, whereas previously I had always been able to take any opportunity that came along. Previously, too, I had only ever had myself to look after and I had never particularly felt the need for material possessions or luxury. Now, I had demands for school fees and domestic arrangements.

Anyway, despite all my new commitments, I was glad to return to *Game For A Laugh*, albeit briefly. Matthew, Henry and Sarah left and new teams of presenters, including Rustie Lee, Debbie Rix, Martin Daniels and Lee Peck, replaced them but after a while it was decided that *Game For A Laugh* had probably run its course. We felt that it would be better to leave on a natural high, rather than let it die a slow, agonising death, so LWT decided that *Game For A Laugh* was to be closed down after five years on top of the ratings. It was a sad decision and a sad moment but it was also decided that there was still a demand from the viewing public for the practical jokes, of which I was the main exponent. Rising from the ashes like a phoenix, a brand new show was to emerge. This new show had a catchy new name: *Watch Out Beadle's About*!

9

THE PRINCE OF PRANKSTERS IS CROWNED

Game For A Laugh came to its natural end but the producers knew that the public loved the scams and practical jokes, so it was decided that we would make a completely new show, made up entirely of hidden-camera stunts. In 1984, LWT producers were convinced that such a new show could be a massive hit. I had received various tempting offers from the BBC, particularly at the end of *Game For A Laugh*, and I finally made up my mind to leave LWT.

I was due to sign for the BBC the following day but David Bell, who was then in charge of LWT entertainment, took me out for a midnight dinner and said, 'I am only going to tell you this once because it's not good for you to hear. You are a star and we don't want to lose you.' I was very flattered. Then he offered me a raft of other programmes and added that LWT would produce the pilots for any shows I wanted to make. I hadn't considered leaving because of the money. In fact, they were extremely generous to me, although with me they had not only a host, but also a writer.

I listened carefully and decided to stay. I didn't need to

161

turn my calculator upside down in front of any mirrors to work out that this was one of the very few jobs in my life that I hadn't been sacked from! I had been offered a golden handcuffs deal. So, under an exclusive contract, I stayed and developed *Beadle's About*.

My deal with LWT was initially for one year, but the contract eventually rose to a two-year package. The money was tremendous, and suddenly it made me aware of my value to the business. For the first time I had a regular guaranteed income that was very lucrative. A longer-term contract made life so much easier in that I didn't have to worry about the pennies. This was something quite new to me. Despite my considerable domestic responsibilities, it felt strange to be confronted by a very substantial income. I am not an acquisitive person by nature. I don't go shopping a great deal. I have a library and love books – but that's work. I don't spend money on clothes. I've never been particularly flash and I've always deliberately driven discreet cars. I'm not a big nightclubber. So the money didn't rush to my head. I just imagined that, in a couple of years, I'd move into a bigger house and make life more comfortable for my children. I was pleased to be earning and felt confident I would have a few years of success on television, but I saw this mainly as a chance to build up some reserves.

As regards my love of books, they are my one weakness. I adore books, and they are my one weakness. I adore books and, at home, I have built up a substantial library of about 20,000 volumes. If you were to pay full price for every book in my library today, it would probably set you back well over half a million pounds.

I have a large biography section, an enormous crime collection, and in articular, thousands of books reflecting my life-long fascination with the offbeat, the maverick, the unusual and the curious. I keep countless tomes on hoaxes, practical jokes, illusion, fakes and frauds, a huge collection of revenge books and hundreds of volumes on sex – always a good read!

One of my most treasured sections is devoted to circus. And I have many other books on oddities, disasters, earthquakes, shipwrecks, volcanoes and storms, on death, unusual wills, funny epitaphs, how the famous died, and quirky last words. I also collect autopsy reports.

Of all the topics covered by my library, crime is probably the one I have accumulated the most books on, around three thousand. These refer to everything from famous detectives, infamous murder cases, and forensics, to poisonings, body-snatching and cannibalism.

Also on my shelves are books covering radio and television, the history of hidden-camera stunts, quizzes and game shows. These reference books always came in useful for work on TV formats.

Given that the public loved hidden-camera stunts so much, we felt we could generate enough material to sustain a full half-hour *Beadle's About* show. In the end, it ran for eleven series and was sold around the world. *Beadle's About* went to Number One in Australia and even in the Ukraine! At its peak, it was pulling in around seventeen million viewers. Not bad by today's standards!

We already knew the techniques of hidden-camera work but now, instead of coming up with one scam a week, we had to produce *four or five* scams a week for *Beadle's About*. This added up to enormous amounts of pre-production, much thinking, plotting and planning. We'd learned many valuable lessons when casting actors and staging technical tricks, but much hard graft clearly lay ahead.

I have always been annoyed by people accusing me of ripping off *Candid Camera*. This shows an acute disregard for the history of hidden-camera shows. The first one in this country wasn't even called *Candid Camera*; it was actually an Art Linkletter show entitled *People Are Funny*. *Beadle's*

About differs from *Candid Camera* in a very simple way. *Candid Camera* was played out on unsuspecting, unresearched members of the public, for example, setting up a talking lamp-post or making an object in a restaurant move mysteriously. They were very simple practical jokes. They had a shooting ratio of about twenty-five or thirty attempts in order to film one take for transmission. On *Beadle's About*, we generally had *one* go. It was all or nothing. The risk factor was always incredibly high and it's a huge credit to my teams that we achieved so many successes. Also, I always felt *Candid Camera* could be rather cruel as you never really knew whether the person targeted had strolled unawares into their set-up. They might have just visited a funeral parlour, or maybe they had just come out of hospital.

From the start, the *Beadle's About* team had certain premises which made a crucial difference. The first producer was Richard Hershey, who had assembled many of the researchers, directors, designers and sound people who had worked on *Game For A Laugh*, the talent that was to be our backbone.

All humour is cruel and everything is funny, so long as it happens to someone else. But everything on the show was done by invitation and consent. In other words, we were invited to play the joke by loved ones or relatives. *Beadle's About* was set up and recorded by invitation and transmitted with consent. When we were invited to play a joke by the target's loved ones, we wouldn't transmit without the consent of the star. We received a huge amount of mail, about 30,000 letters a year. We had some left over from *Game For A Laugh* too, as well as other ideas that we'd never used. I was loving it all. Very few people have made a full-time career out of something as silly as practical joking and to be recognised as the country's Number One in that field was something I took as a great accolade. *Game For A Laugh* had been my apprenticeship and had established me in the role. *Beadle's About* marked my coronation! I was now the King of Practical Jokes, The Prince of Pranksters.

While we put the people through the mill when we played a practical joke on them, we always consulted their doctor first to see if there was a medical reason why we shouldn't go ahead. We also spoke to their family and workmates and found out as much as possible about them before working out how far we could go. What we were looking for was their vulnerable point. Vulnerability can be excessive pride, a zealousness, maybe someone who's obsessive about cleanliness. What did they care most about? With men the areas are obvious – cars and money. Women are far more subtle. Their weak points are usually vanity and children. Blend truth and falsehood around those elements and you have the basis for a good scam. When these areas are at stake people suffer sense of humour failure, lose all sense of propriety and become unreasonable. Perfect conditions for us to play.

Beadle's About made people laugh, yet I was often accused of cruelty. What most people don't know is that, when we've allowed loved ones behind the scenes to watch the action, nine times out of ten they've urged us to go in *harder*! I usually declined. You could accuse me of being cruel if I had picked on someone with a genuine phobia, which I would *never* do. If someone was scared of spiders and we had created a joke that involved them being in a room with spiders, that wouldn't be funny. The key to the success is that I have an absolute fascination with people and I am very curious as to what makes them tick.

You only have to visit a British holiday camp to witness what happens when the resident comedian calls for volunteers. People rush up on stage and seem more than happy to make fools of themselves. It's an opportunity to show off. Every Friday night, pubs across Britain hold karaoke and sing-along evenings. I have always presented and produced people shows because I feel I have a flair and instinct for knowing what the public like. It's because I have been, and still am, myself a member of the public. I am not some remote lardy, some lofty actor. I just know how people like to enjoy themselves. I was probably helped by my working-class childhood, growing up on a council estate, then toiling in factories, taking driving jobs, working behind bars and portering in hospitals. I still feel very much working-class. I am very proud to be working-class.

Although I played a few practical jokes on celebrities, they never really worked as well as the ones I played on the public. Celebrities never forget the fact that they are 'on'. They are in showbusiness most of the time and the very word 'showbusiness' tells you that it's their business to show themselves. I'll happily watch Noel Edmonds deliver a *Gotcha!* on the famous. Some of them have been brilliantly funny but, in my view, many failed to reach the peak of laughter created by the common man striving valiantly to extricate himself from our human bear-traps. Celebrities remain very aware of their image at all times, so they never lose control completely and are never really themselves, whereas members of the public will fight their corner at a very basic level. When they become territorial, one can create confusion, which can be very funny.

The audience tends to sit at home saying things like, 'They wouldn't catch me like that . . . I wouldn't do that.' But when they watch a six-minute stunt, they don't know about the forty minutes we cut out, the time we spent building the set-up before springing the trap. It's during the build-up that the person is snared psychologically.

Beadle's About brought me my fair share of adverse publicity. I am quite capable of taking criticism and I have, in fact, been known to act on constructive feedback in the past, when a TV critic has said something that could make a programme better. But *Beadle's About* didn't really attract criticism. I attracted personal abuse. I'm not all that thick-skinned and I can be bruised and battered like the next person. If you ask me, 'Was I really wounded?', then no. But I didn't enjoy the rough ride. The abuse I was receiving was very personal. I'm not a particularly vain person either but they called me fat and bulgy-eyed and deformed. And they were right – so what am I supposed to do about it? On reflection, the things they said didn't hurt me, they angered me. More to the point, I used to feel very angry about the critics' lack of knowledge of the programme and their failure to even attempt to understand it. Undeniably, *Beadle's About* became the Rolls-Royce of its genre and it didn't happen by chance. It earned that reputation through a great deal of hard work and creative thinking.

The best thing about *Beadle's About* was that everyone regarded working on it as tremendous fun. Even though the researchers wouldn't sleep for nights before their items, we all loved the pressure. I'd like to think that if you talked to any of the teams that have worked with me that they will say it was tremendous fun.

The production schedule was gruelling. The full team would start in March, but the previous December I would be mapping out the shows with the producer. A list of about two hundred ideas for different scams would be whittled down to about one hundred, then we would put them to the team. They in turn would have gone through all the letters we had received. These were discussed openly in the office, although our weekly planning meetings, attended only by senior production executives, were absolutely top secret. The office received 30,000 letters at the very beginning of each series and this enormous postbag was channelled through our two associate producers. They'd classify them, making notes in the computer about the type of scam. The one word we *never* used was 'victim'. We were going to make these people stars, so we called them 'punters'.

Anyone who thinks *Beadle's About* was a cheap show to engineer, a bit of a hit-and-miss affair, can forget it. *Beadle's About* was one of the most expensive shows on television. So meticulous was our planning that we once devoted a full eighteen months to preparing and plotting another set-up. The average cost of a stunt would probably be £10,000 to £12,000, but some cost much more, even double. The most expensive single stunt we ever staged cost over £80,000. When we went out to film, there would probably be between thirty-five and forty people involved, as well as a dozen vehicles and three or four cameras.

I am always asked how we hid all the cameras. We improvised a great deal with new technology and miniature cameras. We created a 'nipple cam', which we hid in the button of a denim jacket, where the breast button normally goes. We also concealed a camera in a pair of glasses, which worked extremely well, with miniature lenses fixed to the centre of a pair of Buddy Holly spectacles and our tiny dot camera was hidden in the frames. The Buddy Holly glasses were developed by an English inventor and I have suggested that they be used in autopsy reports, at scene-of-accident investigations and by insurance assessors.

By using remote control tripods we no longer needed to operate cameras. This technical innovation enabled us to put them in silly places, such as bookshelves, behind flowers, inside TV monitors. But the real question was not where you hid the cameras, rather how you recorded the sound.

The sound team was extremely important and often the secret behind the success of *Beadle's About*. Whilst the pictures are relatively easy to film and the cameras are sophisticated – and we did employ some very clever tricks to hide cameras – the most important part of *Beadle's About* was the sound because we could never put microphones on people. Our sound man John Clifton, who sadly died two years ago, was absolutely the best in the business. His brilliant, outstanding and innovative work on *Beadle's About* was never fully publicly acknowledged. Our actors would carry radio mikes on clipboards, under their shirts, in their hats. If you study a *Beadle's About* stunt, you will see somebody lean a certain part of his body towards the star of the stunt, and that's where the microphone is hidden. We have also turned telephones into microphones.

We once staged a very funny scam in a launderette, in Balham, South London. A guy went into the launderette and put his washing in, and all the machines went crazy. Foam started spewing everywhere. It was hysterical because I came in dressed as a frogman. The snag was that the noise of the machines making the foam drowned out all the sound. In the end, we had to cut the item right down because of the lack of a decent soundtrack.

If you were to walk into the street and ask a pedestrian to name four people who make them laugh, they'd probably come up with the Jimmy Tarbucks, the Bob Monkhouses of this world. Ask them to recall a single joke and they'd be struggling. Beadle wouldn't be on that laughter list. But if you asked them to name their favourite *Beadle's About* stunt, they'd all have one. They would remember it vividly.

One of my favourite stunts involved the berserk sausage-making machine. Producers love sausage machines and potter's wheels. They can be very phallic. It's a guaranteed laugh to see a woman trying to handle out-of-control sausages. I also enjoyed the exploding baked beans stunt, which involved using high-pressure air hoses to pump gallons of beans everywhere. To me, there is something about baked beans exacting their revenge and putting the wind up people, which is really hysterical.

We also had the idea of a nun visiting a dating agency. We fixed up our girl punter a job at the agency, and asked her to guide the nun (an actress) through her first date. At the

169

end I came in disguised as an Italian Lothario and started making eyes at the nun. Our punter tried to protect the nun from my leering!

I especially enjoyed the day the Queen arrived at a greengrocer's and all the royal corgies jumped out of a huge limousine. The punter, working as a shop assistant, came out to sell her oranges and cabbages through the blacked-out windows of the car while the naughty corgies escaped. The Queen in the limousine was actually me, though all you could see was my gloved hand. Inside the car, I was even made up to look like the Queen, wearing the full royal regalia in case the punter peeped through. That was very funny.

Mighty Mo came from Peckham in South London and was a real fireball. She lived next door to a bookmaker's that didn't have a lavatory. All day, gamblers used to pop out and pee at the side of her house. Obviously, Mo became very upset about this, so we very kindly arranged for some men's urinals to be *nailed* to the wall at the side of her house! Her real name was Mo but we nicknamed her Mighty Mo because her reaction was so spectacular. She went absolutely crazy, racing out without her teeth in. She fiercely fought her corner with 'rich' language. It was marvellous!

Audacity can sometimes be the best method of deception. In one stunt, in a fake electronics store, we had difficulty hiding a microphone in front of the punter. So we stuck a really big microphone on the counter and just hung a 'For Sale' notice on it. And we always made sure the brightest lights were reserved for areas *away* from the main action. That helped to distract the punter and led them to believe something far more important was happening elsewhere.

Probably the funniest moments on screen are what we called the 'reveals', where I make my entrance and reveal it's a *Beadle's About* stunt. Over the years, I employed many different disguises and devices to develop this moment into a triumph of comedy. The ones I always enjoyed most were the slow burns. The star has been so wound up that they fail to recognise me. I often removed wigs, fake moustaches, placed a large hand-microphone under their noses – and *still* they failed to twig it was me! The longer it's taken for them to realise they're on television, the funnier it is. I've watched studio audiences start with a laugh that's gradually built to hysterics and finally sent the sound needle in the engineer's box into overload as the punter struggled to work it out!

Keeping the punter on camera at the precise moment of the reveal has often been tricky. It has sometimes required me to hold them, or literally lift them back into view. Once they realise it's me, I'll dance with them as they twist and turn, and clutch them in a frenzied tango. The most frequent reaction is for people to cover their faces with their hands. They'll also flap their arms wildly, or hug me to death with relief! Some are completely dumbstruck, others claim they 'knew all along!' Some wave at the camera and say, 'Hi, Mum!' and there are those who resolutely refuse to believe it's happened to them, even when I'm standing beside them. Early on we developed the technique of keeping the cameras rolling *after* the reveal and after the punter thought it was all over. Often that's when the punter was completely offguard and at his or her most expressive. These priceless shots were edited in later.

I developed the world's simplest but most effective technique for the reveal. It requires me to do nothing. You probably think I'm pretty good at that! But it may surprise you to learn that doing nothing requires nerve and experience. I would just produce the microphone and say nothing. Eventually the punter always said something. And, whatever they said, it would be gold! Meanwhile, I

171

always knew we could edit away the gaps and silences later. If I've ever had a dispute with a producer, then nine times out of ten it's been because I felt they edited the reveal too tightly.

For my money, the comedy generated by real people in absurd situations has produced greater laughs than most of the professionally scripted comedy I've watched over the years. I may have been classed as a menace to society but I think I've also produced some of the funniest escapism television ever seen on British screens. Immodest? Yes. True? I really believe it.

Over the years, we were always tempted to make our stunts more and more elaborate. But I always argued that the scale is not as important as the laughs. Bleeped-out blue language guarantees a laugh. I've even been known to bleep out quite *innocent* language to spice up a stunt! I argue we are writing comedy, not recording a fly-on-the-wall documentary, and make no excuse or apology for taking liberties with reality. It makes the public laugh – and that's my aim and function.

Frustration was often one of the key elements of a stunt. To watch a victim frustrated by a 'jobsworth' is hysterical because we've all been there! Our supporting cast of actors were enormously important. Their primary role was to keep the action going, like audience hecklers to a stand-up comic. They teased, cajoled and shocked, in order to make punters more and more confused and even more angry. The public just love watching people lose their rag. The more ridiculous our actors, the more exasperated the punter, the bigger the laughs. The actors were taught that the more reasonable the punter grew, the more unreasonable they must act. On the other hand, when the punter began to appear angry, our actors would back off, becoming sympathetic. This technique not only confused the punter, but added to the comedy. They were also taught never to answer a question, only to ask them. This kept the pressure on the punter, allowing him or her no thinking time. Very important! Another trick we taught our actors was to keep their backs to the cameras in order to highlight the star. The actors were taught to always listen and to improvise wherever possible, and above all, never to interrupt the punter. They were the stars.

Nonetheless, it could often be extremely difficult to arouse punters. Viewers always say, 'Good job you didn't try that on me. I would have really let you have it.' In most cases, this is untrue. It took time and patience before punters really let go. Of course, we didn't transmit the build-up. We cut straight to the action. The most difficult people to catch were the unpredictable ones, people who didn't necessarily think logically – but remember, we knew *everything* about our punters, often more than their family, friends and neighbours. And, despite what people think, big men are not the most dangerous punters. But watch out for small men and large ladies! They respond far more quickly and loudly. Perhaps men fear physical retaliation, whereas women war with words, not expecting blows.

A cracker involved the husband and wife who visited a military museum. He decided to climb inside a tank, which he then started up – and proceeded to demolish twelve cars right in front of her – while the wife was screaming at him to stop. Another marvellous stunt involved our *human jingle machine*, when we enticed a guy into an office to act as an answerphone. He was sent to us via an employment agency to a sound-recording studio, which, it turned out, manufactured personalised answerphone jingles. The snag was, the machines broke down and it meant that our punter had to sing all the jingles – *live*! Each of the incoming phone lines registered a different type of music – rock, ballad, disco – and he had to answer the phone in all these different styles. He did brilliantly! The story had a wonderfully

173

happy ending. The punter had a long-lost brother, from whom he had become separated. Our guy was convinced he was the sole survivor of his family, but, by amazing coincidence, his brother was watching *Beadle's About* and recognised him. Shortly afterwards they were reunited.

If somebody wears a very bad wig, it's almost impossible not to stare, isn't it? I defy you to look into the *eyes* of somebody who's wearing an obvious wig. We sent our punters to what we said was a very important interview in an office where they had to meet a consultant, played by our actor in a wig which was specially rigged to start crawling round his head! The wig moved more and more and looked sillier and sillier. The punters tried not to laugh as the actor looked up and asked, 'Is there a problem?' That really creased me up!

Beadle's About became famous for stunts involving clairvoyants, which were fun because we already knew everything about the person in question. We could disguise an actress as a clairvoyant with a head-dress, and sneak an earpiece into whatever she was wearing, then hide the family in the room next-door. Then, the punter could ask the clairvoyant any question at all, like. 'What colour is my settee at home?', and the family would microphone through the correct answer. On one stunt, we had convinced our punter that the clairvoyant genuinely had supernatural powers. The clairvoyant then piped up, 'I think I can see your husband now. I can also project your thoughts on to this television screen.' We had planted the husband in the local pub with this girl (our punter's best friend). As soon as they knew they were on, they started canoodling and being lovey dovey with each other! The wife went bonkers, to put it mildly. 'So *that's* where my husband's gone. He's with my best friend!' she fumed. 'You wait till I get home!' After a while, the husband arrived with an apology to his wife, and said he was going to have to go out that night. His wife really went for him! She was absolutely furious with him – until I walked in.

We managed to convince other punters that they had tremendous supernatural powers themselves. By looking at objects, we told them, they could make the objects explode, move, fall over, or collapse. This, once again, involved elaborate props and it was very funny to watch the reactions. We even convinced one chap that he was God! Think about it! . . . God! He'd just arrived *as a courier* to deliver a package, to the Order of the Crystal Palace, this strange cult we dreamt up. When he arrived at the building, everybody stared at him and started bowing. He gradually realised that they saw him as their Messiah. As the chanting went on, he began to enjoy this. 'According to the Book of the Prophets,' they told him, 'you would arrive in a black chariot.' He had turned up in a taxi! We concocted a list of other convincing reasons why he could be the Messiah. Finally, they pulled back some curtains and there, on the wall, was a portrait of the Messiah. And it was him! The women members of our cult went hysterical. The expression of pleasure on his face was something to behold!

Another woman who went potty was the punter who came to work in our bogus model agency. She kept hearing screams and giggles from the lovely, bikini clad, semi-nude women next door. They kept coming out and talking about the photographer, saying what a dish he was and how naughty he was too. Gradually, the lady began to realise the girls were talking about her husband. Then, just as she happened to be holding a pencil with two hands, the husband appeared. She had a look of thunder on her face as he said, 'Hi darling, what are *you* doing here?' She gritted her teeth and snapped the pencil clean in half!

I think everybody who's worked on *Beadle's About* over the years would agree that there is one absolutely outstanding stunt – the alien, the most expensive, risky and bizarre stunt we could ever hope to get away with. This was so expensive I remember going to my executive producer and pleading the case. I said, 'This is a high-risk show. You have to let us do it.' He asked about our contingency plan if it failed. There wasn't one, but they still allowed us to go ahead.

We planned to land a meteorite, out of which would step an alien. Could we convince somebody that an alien had landed in their garden, we wondered. We tried our luck in Dorset, on an unsuspecting farmer's wife. We recruited the help of the Royal Marines, the local fire brigade, the police force and the coast guard. We built this enormous meteorite, twelve foot long by eight feet high and the husband of the woman punter actually excavated a huge hole in his garden for us to place it in before she came home. Inside were two technicians who had to wear aqua lungs because of the smoke belching out.

The punter had been appearing in a pantomime as one of the singers and returned to find this smoking meteorite in her garden. We reassured her that none of the livestock was harmed and that all her family was safe. Then we convinced her that the meteorite hadn't landed by accident. Meteorites always tended to cluster into areas of creativity, we told her. Was she a creative person, we enquired. 'Yes,' she replied, 'I do a bit of singing,' and she began to sing to the meteorite, which immediately started throbbing and smoking. Following some huge explosions, an alien stepped out. Her conversation with the alien – which contained the immortal line 'Would you like a cup of tea?' – was, without doubt, one of the funniest things I have ever seen on television.

Beadle's About became such a cult show that there were many genuinely disastrous occasions when people really begged for it to be a Beadle stunt. When I *didn't* turn up and they realised theirs was a *real* disaster, their day was ruined! At least when Beadle arrives, everything is restored to normal. The show's fame became a two-edged sword. There was the pig farmer, upset when a government inspector started photographing his farm in North Humberside, who grabbed the camera, pulled out the film and pinned the official to the side of his car. 'Go and bother somebody else,' he growled. He was accused of obstructing a health and safety executive and, in his defence, he claimed he thought it was a *Beadle's About* stunt. Two Irish workmen in Watford were phoned by someone claiming to be Jeremy Beadle, who told them they had to dig up a brand new patio in the garden nearby. So, unbelievably, these two workmen did dig up the new £2,000 patio. In court they claimed I was their defence.

At the end of its life, *Beadle's About* was the longest continually running hidden-camera show of all time, anywhere in the world. It ran for eleven series from 1986 with specials and extra late-night shows. Like all television programmes, its natural life drew to a close. It was felt it needed a rest. The papers claimed, of course, that Beadle was going to be axed, that I had been snubbed and that, at last, the public could breathe a sigh of relief and sleep easy in their beds. While I was disappointed, I am professional enough to recognise that a show can't go on and on forever. The alien stunt, for my money, was the greatest hidden-camera stunt done anywhere in the world – and I have seen most of them.

Since *Beadle's About* ended, more and more people have asked, 'When is it coming back?' There have, of course, been many copycat shows and I wish them all the best of luck. Don't be surprised if *Beadle's About* does come back in some form or another in the future. There'll always be room for a hidden-camera comedy show on television and I think, with our team's experience, we could still supply the best. Yes, I do miss it. But, of course, the end of *Beadle's About* wasn't the end of Beadle. Because again, another door had opened for me and I was already doing what

177

turned out to be another enormously successful show, *You've Been Framed!*

After eleven years of *Beadle's About* and five years of *Game For A Laugh*, for sixteen years, I have been synonymous with practical joking. For sixteen years, I was considered the best. Even if I was to live to be a hundred, I still think that, in my obituary, I will be recognised as one of the great practical jokers TV has known. I am quite proud of that. I will continue to work with practical jokes. It may be that I won't actually be on camera but I'll never lose the ability to deliver them. Let's say my crown is tucked away in a little box, waiting to be taken out and dusted off at some future date.

And importantly over the years I made a lot of friends on *Beadle's About*. They were a great team and I owe them a lot. Apart from my family, few things in life are more important to me. And I like to show loyalty to my friends – I have always done so, thanks to a special lady named Joyce, who had been a great influence in my life.

I first met Joyce Mayes in 1973, when she was about sixty-two and I was about twenty-five. At the time, I regularly drank in a Fuller's pub in West London, round the corner from my home. I was heavily into CAMRA, the Campaign for Real Ale, and I fell into a routine where I would go to this pub every night and consume five pints of very strong beer. Hardly surprisingly, I started to balloon quite seriously. Up until that time, I had been quite skinny, and had a twenty-eight-inch waist. With all that beer, I shot up to fifteen-and-a-half stone, which for a five-foot-eight-inch guy, is fat! My waist went up to forty-two inches, and forty-four at one point.

I enjoyed a nodding acquaintance with this old lady. Rumours had it that her husband was a very miserable man indeed, notoriously irritable and unapproachable, but I grew to know them both quite well. Joyce turned out to be the most extraordinary woman. She was an absolute delight. She became rather pleased with me – because I was the only person that could make her husband laugh. She was born in Canada, in a house on the prairies, right in the middle of nowhere. It had a grid reference – but no name. Her mother was a photographer and so was her father. When her father died, Joyce learned to be a photographer too, and she and her mother came over to England in the 1930s. They bought an old Ford and drove all over England, taking photographs of their travels and keeping a scrapbook, which, many years later, Joyce passed on to me as a gift. To this day it remains one of my most treasured possessions.

Joyce was exceptionally kind and very wise. When her husband died, she was left on her own and I used to take her out every week. This little frail old lady was like a small sparrow compared to me but I used to take her round all the nightclubs in Soho every Friday and this went on for years.

Joyce had a very simple philosophy. She neatly summed up her outlook on the world with one wonderfully wise piece of advice: 'Let your conscience be your guide . . . and feed the birds every day.'

I think that is such a refreshing and fulfilling approach to life. It's about being honest to yourself and your values, and equally about being generous, thoughtful and kind to others. Maybe Joyce borrowed it from Pinocchio, or Mary Poppins, but nevertheless, its simplicity has great substance.

About a week after Joyce died in 1985, Sue took me to the end of the garden and showed me a little treehouse she had built. It was a birds' feeding rest, and at the bottom of it was erected a bronze engraving in honour of Joyce. It read: 'Let your conscience be your guide . . . and feed the birds every day.'

I am basically an extremely private person by nature, even though I wear a very public face. I am quite secretive and I don't tend to share my problems, although a lot of people share their problems with me. I have acted as an emotional sounding board many times and I have always been very sensitive to other people's anxieties.

My friends are incredibly importanmt to me. In fact, I was once asked on a radio show how I wanted my own epitaph to read. I said all I want on my tombstone is: 'Ask His Friends'.

10

HOW MY NAME
GOT IN THE FRAME

In 1982, I was offered my first professional pantomime at Lewisham Theatre, where I played Simple Simon in *Jack and the Beanstalk*. I devised some great audience participation routines, one of which stars a rabbit. It involves inviting kids and, unbeknown to them, their parents (disguised in giant rabbit suits) up on stage and is both hilarious and heart-warming. I once described this rabbit routine to the great Ralph Edwards, creator of *Truth or Consequences*, *This Is Your Life* and *What's My Line?*, who fell about laughing. 'That is one of the best routines I have ever heard,' he said. I am hugely proud of the compliment to this day.

Also starring in the panto were Lulu, the famous Radio Two disc jockey Tony Brand, Bonnie Langford, George Sewell and Henry McGee, who used to work with Benny Hill. They expected me to sing and dance; trouble is, I have Van Gogh's ear for music and I am completely cack-footed. Whenever I reached the songsheet at the end of the show, I used to pull members of the audience up on stage to do it for me. I love audience participation anyway.

I learned a valuable lesson from George Sewell. Panto

181

can be very hard work and the routine extremely grinding. One of the things I hate most in life is routine and the idea of doing the same thing, day in day out, is absolute hell. So, to liven things up, I often played naughty little practical jokes – maybe some props would be misplaced, maybe when I was due to come on stage left, I would make my entrance instead stage right. It would confuse everybody, and I thought it was quite amusing.

One day, I sprang a joke on George. He was cast as the baddie and for that role, in panto, it is quite important that the actor keeps fairly strictly to the script, otherwise the story starts to fall apart. But, I was a bit naughty with George. I deliberately confused my lines to him, so that every time he said something to me, I would change all my responses so that I was able to change the logic of what he was saying. George handled it brilliantly and I came off stage laughing. But George came off after me – *fuming*. He was furious. 'That was extremely unprofessional of you,' he exploded in a rage. 'Don't you understand that the baddie has to stay in character? You can't break the fantasy. It may have been funny to you, but it was completely confusing the audience. Don't you *ever* do that again!' So I learned two lessons that day. The panto baddie's dialogue is not to be messed with – and secondly, neither is George Sewell.

Kids at pantos are great fun. I was once singing a song with some children when this little boy came up on stage. I asked, 'What's your name?' He answered that correctly. Then I said, 'And are you a boy or a girl?' He said, 'I am a boy.' Then I said, 'And how do you *know* that?' And he paused, and thought about it for a bit, and then answered me back, 'Because I am wearing a tie.'

Playing panto is not all sheer joy, of course. You work under tight constrictions. You arrive at the theatre at around noon every day, and you don't leave until eleven o'clock at night. I'll have it written into my panto contracts that I will only wear one outfit throughout the performance because I hate dressing and changes of costumes are a real bore. I will never know how my good friend Matthew Kelly, who plays a brilliant dame, manages so many complicated costume changes. I also make sure my panto costumes have a simple track-suit style with an elasticated belt and an easy-to-wear top. I normally do so much running around in and out of the audience, chasing people and larking about, I tend to lose huge amounts of weight!

I have always liked to give people breaks and help them out because I have appreciated similar gestures on my behalf in the past. It's also very rewarding to help someone when they're starting out in their career. One year, I was doing panto in Hastings and in the cast there was a young girl of about fifteen named Samantha Janus. She was tall and leggy and had a great singing voice. I arranged for her to get work at TV-AM in a singing spot, which I thought would be great for her career. But she was very young and displayed some real prima donna antics, complaining that her costume wasn't ready, and so on. She overestimated her importance and began to get under the skin of some of the older professionals in the cast, who were solid pros.

I did, at one point, put her in her place with a reminder that other members of the cast had been in the business a great deal longer. But the happy ending to this story is that she finished our panto and developed into a very popular and warm-hearted individual and of course went on to enjoy huge success. So, a lesson for anybody starting out: learn from the pros and don't think you are the bee's knees until you have earned it.

What I enjoyed most about work in panto was the chance to appear with pros on stage. Then I suddenly received an offer out of the blue which was to make one of my childhood dreams come true. I always wanted my children to enjoy live entertainment. And I don't just mean poncing

183

down to the Old Vic or going to some swanky alternative theatre soirée, but also going to the bingo, to nightclubs and discos, the circus, pantomime and exhibitions. So I took Cassie and Bonnie to see Gerry Cottle's Circus and we loved the show. Afterwards, we went back to say well done to everybody, which is professional etiquette. In Gerry, I found a real kindred spirit. He's a remarkable showman and there are very few showmen left today.

Gerry and I really hit it off and he invited me to his home, where he keeps his incredible collection of circus memorabilia. Then Gerry rather recklessly turned to me and said, 'How would you like to be the ringmaster in my circus?' I leaped out of my seat! After having admired the circus throughout my childhood, the idea of being on the inside, seeing how the stars of the circus *really* worked, was a fantastic opportunity, an incredible learning experience I desperately wanted to take on.

So I jumped at Gerry's offer. We put in a few trial runs. I went out on the road with the circus, met all the turns, and learned about the routine. Circus people work very, very hard. For any youngster reading this dreamily, being in a circus is a *very* tough life. You really have to love it with a passion. Merely possessing the skills for the job isn't enough. The demands mean that one minute you'll be performing a triple somersault off a trapeze, and the next you'll be selling toffee apples. After that, you'll be sweating buckets struggling to put up a tent, and then you'll be mucking out the horses' stables – or the elephants' quarters!

I know many people object to seeing animals in circuses and there is a huge lobby against the use of performing animals. But, having worked in the circus myself and having seen at first hand how the animals are treated, all I can say is that, in my experience, the animals are looked after incredibly well. If you are going to train a wild cat and are brutal to it, then you risk suffering the consequences later.

Cats have memories! You'll be in big trouble.

In the course of my ringmaster's duties, I have heroically stepped into a big cats' cage once or twice. Lions aren't quite so terrifying because they are basically very lazy. One of the best lion acts in Britain is staged by ringmaster and lion-tamer Martin Lacey, who generates a huge amount of comedy from the fact that his lions are so incredibly lazy. They won't do what he commands them, and never do what they are supposed to. It's a wonderful and very entertaining routine. I have been in with Martin's lions – only the laundryman knew how I felt at the time!

Once I risked life and limb to take part in a photo shoot with tigers. I entered a cage with four tigers, and strangely it felt rather warm in there. Tigers are very different beasts from lions, and are always on the move, always on the look-out. I was posing for a quick photograph, when suddenly the trainer stepped niftily in between me and the tiger and said in a very sincere voice, 'I think you should edge back now . . .' I was only too pleased to 'edge back'. My precise body movements could be described in slightly more energetic vocabulary. That night most of 'the smell of fear' at the circus came from Yours Truly! The tamer in charge of those tigers didn't have to explain to me what was going on because suddenly that enormous tiger just *looked at me*. In criminal slang, when somebody is about to lose control, or turn violent, they shoot what is colloquially known as 'a hundred-yard stare' where they look at you but don't see you. They are looking way beyond you, and you twig in an instant that you have to shift out of their way smartish. The big cat gave me a hundred-yard stare, the only difference being that I was standing only about ten feet away from the tiger at the time! By the way, I do wish that tiger had cleaned his teeth. He had terribly foul breath . . . (Note: it's easy to throw insults from behind the safety of my computer keyboard!)

Martin Lacey used to put his head inside the tiger's mouth. And at Wembley a woman who worked an act with crocodiles placed her head in the croc's mouth. People actually turned away rather than see her do it. Crocodiles have been known to crush the hulls of river cruisers! On Gerry's circus, we also had an elephant called Rani, who once co-starred with me on *Game For A Laugh*. Working with Rani again was a wonderful reunion, and we established a great routine. Before the elephants appeared in the ring, I would call a husband and wife out of the audience. I would say to the wife, 'I would like you to go through those curtains over there and help us with our next act,' and she would dutifully disappear backstage. Then I would turn to the husband and ask him to lie down on his back in the centre of the ring and I'd say, 'We are going to try a little trick now. Does your wife love you?' He'd reply, 'Yes!' Fine. 'Good,' I'd say, 'Well, that's all right, because I would like you to be reunited with your wife . . .' and in would stride Rani the elephant – with the guy's wife seated on top of her back.

Then, Rani would walk slowly towards the guy, who was still lying in the middle of the ring. I'd shout out reassuringly, 'Don't worry, it won't hurt . . . *me!*' Rani would then walk right *over* him, apparently steered expertly by his wife on top. Rani very gently lifted one leg up over the guy's chest and stepped down on the other side. The expressions on the faces of both the husband and the wife were always magical. The amazing thing about elephants, considering their size, is that they are the most sure-footed of animals. Mind you, I've tried myself. And I can tell you, when you see this bloody great elephant walking right over the top of you, you start to seriously wonder whether you are in the right business!

One day Gerry asked me, 'If you could choose to work with any act in the world, which would you choose?' I immediately replied 'Hoppy's Unrideable Mules,' and no sooner had I spoken than my wish was granted.

I would make my entrance into the circus ring and offer anybody in the audience a bottle of champagne if they could stay seated on the back of one of four mules. Of course everybody wanted to have a go. These mules are sensational because they are trained in a special way. If you try to mount them, they put their heads down so you fall off straightaway. If the rider wised up to that, and you tried to sit further back, the mule would rear up on its hind legs and drop you off the back. If you did manage to mount them, they would start bucking, then suddenly stop, then gallop, then stop. You'd be thrown off instantly, whatever you tried. Also the mules would love to run around the ring, so that whenever a member of the audience did try to leap on, the mules would just race off.

There was not a remotest chance of successfully riding these mules but people would keep on trying. The mule pack leader, Hoppy himself, sat in the audience until the second act, when he would come on shouting, 'I want a go!' His wife, who was also planted in the audience, would come out next and try to stop him, and there would be all sorts of fun and games between the two of them. She'd scream, 'Don't be foolish!' and he'd shout back, 'But I want to have a go!' then, he'd lose his trousers. Finally, when he did manage to sit on them, the way he rode those mules was just sensational. It is simply hysterical to watch. It's the most wonderful act.

I had wonderful times with Gerry Cottle and also with other circuses. I came up with an idea to produce a TV show featuring the skills of dare-devils, which Gerry and I pitched to LWT. The plan was to gather the world's finest, most death-defying acts and present them all together in a one-off spectacular. It eventually ended up as a spectacular one-off show called *Beadle's Dare Devils*, which featured some of the most frightening acts you have ever seen in your life! These included a trapeze artist who went through his entire routine, suspended beneath a high-speed helicopter flying over London's River Thames, hanging on to a rope by his teeth! We had a juggler who tossed chainsaws, and a guy who managed to cross a tightrope on a penny farthing bicycle. There was also the strong man who had a truck drive over him while he was lying down on a bed of nails. For his finale, he also caught a cannonball, fired straight at him from a cannon! Another of my daredevil favourites featured Gary Lee's flaming dive of death. He wore a special, flame-resistant suit as he climbed sixty feet and set fire to himself, then dived off on to a mattress on the ground. Unfortunately, Gary injured himself on the day we filmed. Ironically he tripped over a tent pole and hurt his ankle!

I was the one who nearly tripped up and came a cropper when it came to the birth of my next big show on ITV. The stumbling block this time was a well-known star, not of the circus ring, but of the small screen. In 1988, I hosted a new series called *People Do the Funniest Things*, a clip show featuring items from around the world – celebrities when they were children, animal clips, out-takes, cock-ups, practical jokes. The format was an instant hit and won seventeen million viewers.

Introducing the clips, I would play various tricks on the audience. Instead of just delivering a link, I would involve the audience in some sort of scam, such as blowing up air pipes, producing snakes, or collapsing sets. Another element featured out-takes of actors shooting advertisements that went wrong, which Dennis Norden had been doing for years on *It'll Be Alright on the Night*. His show was extremely popular, and also a worldwide seller, and he objected to *People Do the Funniest Things* on the grounds that it was eating into material that he considered *exclu-*

sively his. Although only about 20 per cent of our clips were out-takes, the powers that be listened to Dennis and it was decided that our series would be dropped. I could see Dennis's argument, although I think that he was being a little bit precious, I accepted the decision.

Inadvertently, though, Dennis led to my next success. One element of our show that I'd bought the rights to was a Japanese format whereby members of the public would send in home videos of disasters they'd filmed on their own camcorders. As an alternative, I offered this to LWT as my next project, adding that I thought it was a fantastic idea. I have often found that my ideas are in advance of the market and it can take a long time to convince people to listen. And this format too was turned down, for several reasons. The powers that be weren't keen on a foreign clip show and they said there weren't enough camcorders in Britain to make it a home-grown hit. LWT was also about to launch its bid to keep its ITV franchise and, because they already had a number of existing clip shows, they didn't want another one. I argued that the camcorder industry was expanding at a rapid rate of knots, and tried to interest other people, but failed. I relinquished the rights, which went to America, where a chap called Vin di Bono bought the rights and made a series called *America's Funniest Home Videos*. It proved an enormous success and was said to be President Bush's favourite TV programme.

Spotting the huge business the show was generating in America, Action Time, the Manchester-based independent production company with which I had been involved, then bought the UK rights *back* from Vin di Bono, selling them on to Granada TV, who made a pilot. Despite the fact that it was hosted by Richard Madeley, this turned out to be rather weak. It was suggested that I ought to take a look at the show so I went up to Granada and watched the tape. There were many mistakes in it, in my view. The public, I

189

said, just wanted the clips. They'd taken a really simple idea and confused it by adding too much, and although Richard Madeley is a superb professional, he had been miscast.

I filmed a new pilot at Granada. Originally it wasn't intended for transmission to the general public, but, in my view, we pitched it right and I pleaded that we should broadcast it, even though it was a bit rough around the edges. That was the only way we were going to attract any tapes for a series. Although we'd advertised for tapes and had quite a few sent in, up until then we certainly didn't have enough for a series. We'd gathered some American and Japanese tapes but ours needed to have a *British* flavour. Eventually I won the argument and we transmitted the pilot of *You've Been Framed*, with all its faults, in 1989. It was an instant hit. Everybody loved it. The buzz convinced the bosses at Granada, and the ITV network, that they had potentially a big show on their hands, so it was decided that we'd go into immediate production.

I have always argued that there should be a department in television called family entertainment. And there still isn't. There's sport, drama, current affairs, documentaries, children's . . . and light entertainment, but that covers a broad field. Family entertainment would make programmes which the whole family could sit down and enjoy at the same level of pleasure and understanding. The main reason this has never happened is because these formats are the most difficult to establish. Classic examples include *Game for a Laugh*, *The Generation Game*, *Noel's House Party*. *You've Been Framed!* was also an absolutely perfect family show. Parents still come up to me and say that their child is three years old and *You've Been Framed!* is the one show they love watching. We had tapes sent in of children crying when the episode of *You've Been Framed!* ended, and also tapes of babies laughing their heads off. Equally, I have also had high court judges, MPs and captains of industry tell me that *You've Been Framed!* is their favourite show.

Once *You've Been Framed!* was up and running, I took a very hands-on interest in the tone of the clips. I didn't want to see babies' heads under water, and I didn't want the audience to be shocked or to be reminded of unpleasantness. Nevertheless the show was made very democratically by the team. As we viewed tapes I'd sometimes see something that offended my sensitivities, whereas everybody else laughed. I argued that I was not sure it was right for the programme, but if four people are laughing their heads off and you are sitting there stone cold, then who's right?

People have often asked me about the ones that we *didn't* show. 'What about the dirty clips?' The truth is that we didn't really receive any. We were sent countless clips of dogs shagging carpets, bulls and cows mounting each other and various other animal ones, and we also had loads where women's breasts fell out of their clothing – all very tame. One which did raise a few eyebrows featured a guy who set up a video camera in his front room. He was decorating – and that's all it was. The three-hour tape showed him decorating the room, scraping the wallpaper off and so on. The only thing odd about him was that *he was totally stark naked*! At one point, he went out to make a cup of tea, sat down to read the paper, and then he resumed his job. Nothing else happened.

Kids really believed, and continue to believe, that the set house was my real home. When I visit schools, pupils always ask me, 'What's it like to live in a house that turns around?' I always reply that it's fabulous because if I ever want a glass of milk, I just say, 'Milk!' and the house and the milk in the kitchen come to me. They believe this and they love it. I receive hundreds of letters simply addressed to 'Beadle who lives in the round house' and 'Beadle who lives in the house that moves'. They all make it through the post!

Because of the huge size of the postbag on *You've Been*

Framed!, I was unable to view all the tapes that were sent in. We received between 30,000 and 40,000 tapes each year, and employed four full-time people to view them. They logged and listed them, then themed them as 'packages'. Eventually we would come up with a list of about sixty or seventy different packages, such as 'walking into walls' or 'tumbling' or 'water' or 'custard pies'. I would generally view about one hundred tapes before I sat down with the scriptwriter to discuss the various links. For the voiceovers, I'd go into the studio. My philosophy was 'less is more'. Sometimes we were tempted to try to be funnier than the clips, but if the clips are really funny, then you just had to let them breathe.

In my view, the general public make the best scriptwriters in the world. There's a huge amount of talent out there and, in a slightly different context, some of the most hilarious clips the public ever submitted reached me when I presented another ITV show. It sprang from a late-night Radio Two show called *Beadle's Nightcap*. It included an element called Sixty-Second Masterpieces, in which I asked the public to phone in with their own adaptations of the classics, whether they be *Julius Caesar*, *A Tale of Two Cities*, *Alice in Wonderland*, or a war adventure. Some absolutely brilliant material flooded in and I thought we ought to be able to repeat it on television. At the time camcorders were becoming popular in Britain, and *Beadle's Hotshots*, a TV comedy sketch show made by the public on camcorders, took off. On its first screening, the pilot episode attracted a very respectable eight million viewers. On its second showing, it reached twelve million, though sadly the show didn't run for as long as some of my other series.

You've Been Framed! was fantastic to work on but, as before, all things come to an end. I did the show for nine years and it reached Number One in the TV ratings several times. *You've Been Framed!* was a hugely popular, successful and profitable show and I would like to think that it was the most loved family show of its time.

I was coming to a point in my career where I was receiving a number of offers to front many different types of shows. I do have a wide range of interests outside light entertainment, although I must say the thing I enjoy most is hearing laughter as a result of a programme I have made. For sixteen years, I had been under an exclusive contract that prevented me from working with other TV companies, so, the time felt right to move on. I'd enjoyed success with *You've Been Framed!* and likewise with *Beadle's About*, and now I wanted to be released from my exclusive contract. But, of course, when it was announced last Autumn, the newspapers automatically jumped in the air with headlines like 'Beadle's Been Axed', which, as usual, wasn't the case.

It was a very amicable parting and it doesn't mean to say that I won't be working with ITV again. I've clocked up eleven years with *Beadle's About*, five years with *Game For A Laugh*, nine years with *You've Been Framed!* The sobering truth is that the decision to release myself from guaranteed security to take on new challenges – which may or may not be successful – is a major risk. But I love challenges and I'm always excited by change. I reached the point on *You've Been Framed!* where I felt it wasn't dangerous enough, and it wasn't as demanding creatively as *Beadle's About*. I wanted to take on new challenges, develop new formats, work on different projects that would excite my creative buds. And that's just what I have done.

I think the real key to success is being very selective and careful with your choice of people around you. You have to recognise those people who are of real worth. Maybe they're of value to your heart, or to your soul, or to your brain, or just to your prospects. My skill, if I have had any skill at all, is in being a skilled people-picker. Though I have had luck in life I also think much success results from plain bloody hard work. There have been times when I have, literally, gone for days concentrating on projects without sleep. There are many very clever people about and you have to create your own opportunities. You have to believe in yourself, otherwise you will never make it. Most people see problems in their life, but I only see the advantages. I really enjoy opening the shutters in my bedroom every morning and looking out on the day. I always devote a little extra time to this daily ritual. The great thing about living in Britain with such a varied climate is that you never know if you're going to be blessed with bright sunshine, thick fog, snow, rain, hail, or mist. Dull, damp or warm weather, I am always genuinely excited by what the day brings. I love it when somebody rings me up with an idea. Even if I know it's not going to work, I don't tell them that. I highlight its best aspects. I love to see the positive side of things.

My stint in the circus ring for Gerry Cottle didn't mark the last time I was to don the red ringmaster's coat. I very rarely do chat shows on television, and very rarely appear on television at all other than in my own shows. But in 1991 I was asked to present a prize at the British Comedy Awards, and it struck me as an opportunity to squeeze in a plug for Gerry's circus. I agreed with the producers of the show that I would come straight from the circus dressed as ringmaster, and would be allowed to mention the circus.

Jonathan Ross was hosting the awards ceremony. We go back a very long way to Action Time, where he used to work as a researcher. He filmed a couple of pilots with us as a pretend contestant, and I like to think we were quite helpful in landing Jonathan his original show. I knew that Jonathan can cut a fine line with his wit, so I insisted on writing my own introduction. I left the circus wearing my ringmaster's outfit, and was driven in a limousine over to the awards dinner. I was standing backstage, waiting to go on, when I heard my introduction, which was nothing like the piece I had written. It was live TV, and Jonathan's was a very tongue-in-cheek introduction. I was naturally a bit peeved that they had ignored my piece. As I walked on stage, Jonathan's first comment was, 'Mine's a glass of wine,' insinuating that I looked like a wine waiter. I didn't respond. Then he said, 'What have you come as?' Well, I did not intend to tolerate this, live broadcast or not, so I said, 'I've come as Gerry Cottle because I am in his circus and if you're going to be sarkie, I am going to get my plug in!' Jonathan immediately countered by saying, even more sarcastically, 'Well, I'm certainly off to the circus after this.' I pinched the last line, saying, 'I don't think so, Jonathan. They only let talent in,' which prompted a big 'Oooooooh!' from the audience. The press loved it, of course. Our short and sharp exchange received headline billing and became the night that Beadle got the needle and I was rude to Ross. Most interestingly, the papers the next day commented that Jonathan had been very near the knuckle and sarcastic with many of his introductions. It seemed, for once, that the papers were on my side and had decided that Jonathan needed to be put in his place and that I had done a good job. I rarely have a go like that, although I do have a sharp tongue when it's needed.

I was caught on the hop by *somebody else* wearing a red coat in December 1993. That moment will linger much longer in my memory. I was coming to the end of a very busy day. I'd had a late finish the previous night, and I was up and down the country doing various bits and pieces. I'd been to Birmingham earlier, then popped into Swindon, then had to rush back to my children's school carol concert, which was being held in a church in Hampstead in North London, before doing a personal appearance in the evening, about which I was terribly anxious.

Throughout the day, I kept ringing my manager Michael Cohen. (See, I *do* give you a plug in the book, Michael!) I kept asking him, 'Michael what *is* this gig tonight?' He replied, 'Don't worry. All you have to do is go on and be funny for a few minutes. Just go and enjoy yourself.' But I kept asking him for more details. 'You just have to present a couple of awards, that's all,' he insisted. It was very unlike Michael to be so vague, as he is normally very precise and detailed in his briefings.

I turned up for the concert at the church feeling tired and wound up. The place was full. All I really wanted to do was to go home and snatch a couple of hours' sleep before I went out again in the evening. I met Sue, who explained that some of the parents had organised to video a recording of the carol concert and the school nativity play before. So we sat down near the front as the headmistress came up and asked me if I would mind introducing Father Christmas. This came as a complete surprise to me but I said, 'No problem, give me a signal and I'll stand up and bring on Father Christmas for you.'

I sat back down again and noticed something strange. The lights were really professional and very expensive. I turned to Sue, 'Do you know, these lights are amazing. Who's actually making this video?' She replied, 'Oh, just a couple of parents, I think. I hear they are quite rich.' Then, while we were waiting, I noticed that the cameras looked really very expensive too. Somebody in the business, like me, always knows that a very thick television cable is always an outside-broadcast cable, which meant there had to be a TV studio nearby. I found myself looking down at these wires on the floor and began to wonder where they led. They had to be connected to a generator or something . . .

I sat there slightly bewildered until the headteacher called me up to introduce Father Christmas. I climbed up on stage, in front of all the parents and all the kids, to say a few lines.

Now, there is a basic rule in showbusiness called 'short on, long off', which means that whenever you are introduced you always take the shortest route to make your entrance in case the applause doesn't last until you hit your mark. Then you have a 'long off' to milk the applause. I assumed that our Father Christmas was going to do a 'short on', followed by a 'long off'.

I said, 'Ladies and gentlemen, Father Christmas.' But instead of coming in from the side of the stage, Santa made his entrance from right down the back of the church. At this point, all I thought was, 'Blimey, these bloody amateurs don't know what they're up to! What on earth am I doing here? I wish they'd take some advice and let me show them how to produce these events.'

Father Christmas came among the audience going 'Ho! Ho! Ho!' tapping people on the back, smiling and waving. Then he climbed on stage and said 'Well, Jeremy, have you been a good boy this year?' and I replied, 'No!' And I said to myself, 'Oh get on with it, man!' Then Father Christmas, who was wearing the full gear – the bushy white wig, the big red coat and the ample hood – reached into his sack and said, 'Well, I do have a few things in here for you.'

He pulled out a hand-held microphone. I took one look at this piece of equipment and what went through my mind at this point was, 'How can they let this bloody amateur play with this expensive equipment? I bet this old boy doesn't even know how to use it!' So, I sort of turned away . . .

And then Father Christmas pulled out from his sack of presents a gift I shall never forget. It was a very famous red book. And, as he handed it to me, Father Christmas pulled down his hood and said seven terrifying words: 'Jeremy Beadle, tonight, This Is Your Life'. And I was absolutely dumbstruck. Of all the people who should have been cute to TV surprise, it should have been Beadle! There I stood, confronted with all the clues – the professional cameras, the lights, the cables, the microphone – but I never had the

197

slightest notion that mischief was afoot. It was an absolutely wonderful moment. I was in deep shock and I couldn't work it all out. I kept thinking, 'Why me? I haven't done anything special.' Of course, Father Christmas was Michael Aspel, with whom I had worked in the past. I had been a regular guest on his Capital Radio show – and *still* I didn't recognise him! So anybody who thinks they'll never be caught out shouldn't believe it for a single moment.

For the first time in my life, I knew precisely what it felt like to be surprised on television. Malcolm Morris, the producer of *This Is Your Life*, approached me as we were leaving the church. He laughed, 'There we are, Beadle! I told you, one day I'd get you.' I was so knackered and confused that poor Sue thought I was going to have a heart attack! I was still absolutely dumbfounded.

I was suddenly swept away back home and then whisked on to the studio. On *This Is Your Life*, they have what they call 'red star seats' where certain guests sit on the stage after they tell their stories. Then you have other guests who don't make the stage but who sit in the audience. I was told that my show in the studio prompted one of the largest numbers of guests ever in the history of *This Is Your Life*. There were more wonderful people under that roof that night collected together than I could have ever imagined. There was so much talent and warm-hearted kindness and generosity among all my friends. It really was a wonderful occasion.

Normally the *This Is Your Life* team treat their surprises and guests as top secret until the show is broadcast. Rather than call each show the 'Jeremy Beadle show' or the 'Les Dennis show', they give each target a special secret code-word. I later found out that the code name for my show was 'Framed'. But somebody there leaked the story that I had been caught by Michael Aspel to *The Sun* and the whole of the front page next day read, 'Watch Out, Aspel's About: Santa Michael Traps Beadle.'

On only one other famous occasion was I left completely and utterly speechless. I was in the middle of the ghost gag in a pantomime in Leeds. It was a traditional panto routine, where a ghost came out on stage behind you, and the audience, especially the children, shouted at the tops of their voices, 'It's – behind – you!' I would spin around to find that the ghost had vanished, walking behind me to the other side so I would go through the same routine again. The audience screamed, 'It's behind you!' and I'd say, 'Oh, no it's not!' And they'd all go completely crazy, 'Oh, yes it is!' . . . 'Oh, no it's not!' . . . 'Oh, yes it is!' they'd holler back until the roof was raised.

I've always really enjoyed this routine because it whips the audience into a huge frenzy, with everyone screaming at the tops of their voices, and I often milk it for some considerable time. On this particular night, a little boy suddenly stepped out from the audience and came walking down the aisle where I was standing to centre stage. He was knee high to a grasshopper but his face was aglow with a huge look of determination. He stood by the orchestra pit and raised his hand as if to stop me in my tracks. I just *knew*, from all my instincts and years of experience, that this was going to be one of those truly golden moments. *Whatever* he said it was surely going to be a truly heart-warming incident that would steal the show. It had to be fantastic and would be sure to bring the house down.

So I stopped my routine and the musicians ceased playing. The theatre went quiet. I walked downstage slowly and finally reached the front of the footlights opposite this little boy. A profound hush fell over the entire audience. I bent down to hear what this little cherub had to say.

'Yes?' I enquired.

The boy just crossed his arms, frowned and looked up at me sternly. '*Are – you – fucking – deaf?!*'

11

PITFALLS AND PERILS
OF THE FAME GAME

Although I never knew my father, I am aware that he was a newspaper journalist and so it has always struck me as rather ironic that, over the years, I have developed a somewhat strange and strained relationship with the British press.

Fame is a two-edged sword. On the one hand, it has many advantages. If you join the Celebrity Club, suddenly you are automatically on first-name terms with famous people and you can meet your heroes. There are other privileges. If you go to the zoo, you'll be allowed behind the scenes to stroke the animals and cuddle the baby gorillas. When you go to a restaurant, if they're full you are still always guaranteed a table.

But, in my experience, many people who crave celebrity haven't seriously thought about it. Only when you lose your privacy do you realise how valuable it really is. If some people setting off in search of celebrity were to fully understand what it means to suffer the permanent deprivation of privacy, then I think most celebrities would stay anonymous.

Not being comfortable in public places is exhausting. I

have learned to love take-aways and rented videos. I now know what it's like to be a pretty girl walking past a building site full of leering, loutish builders. People often assume that I am both deaf and blind! They wander by me and, in a loud whisper, say, 'It's him!' It very quickly starts to cramp your style. It can put you off your stride when a stranger comes up to you and says, 'Go on, *prove* you're Jeremy Beadle.' It's not that people intend to be rude. I can understand someone wanting to say hello as, after all, they've invited you into their home and expect you to be as welcoming in real life.

Before I acquired 'celebrity', I used to love people-watching, in hotel lobbies or waiting rooms in train stations. Now, I can no longer enjoy that. I have to keep moving otherwise the fans may close in! Although I'm an extrovert and not shy, I *am* a private person and if I don't want to be bothered, then I won't make eye contact. But the disadvantage of walking about face down is that I hit walls!

The poll published in *Punch* magazine where I came second to the Iraqi dictator Saddam Hussein in research to discover 'the most hated man in Britain', has given me endless problems over the years. In fact, when we checked the details, my name was one of only *five* offered to voters. I think Margaret Thatcher and Jonathan Ross were also on the list. And across the nation, a total of merely 225 people were asked to take part in the poll. Meanwhile every newspaper and a million journalists since have asked me the same boring question: 'What's it like to be the most hated man?' When asked what I thought of *Punch*, I would tend to reply, 'Well, at least I make people laugh.' The magazine folded a few issues later.

The royals are no strangers to being misrepresented by the press. Princess Diana understood that well, of course. I remember vividly sharing quite a long conversation with her at a charity function in London. She was a particularly delightful person and I could tell many stories about her personal kindness, gestures that she made very privately without attracting any press attention whatsoever. Diana was genuinely caring and her death meant the loss of somebody who made a huge difference to the lives of many unfortunate people.

People may not realise this but Diana would often visit the Royal Marsden Hospital, in private and without warning, to talk to patients receiving its specialist treatments for cancer. One night, she came in to visit patients in two of the wards. A friend of mine was visiting her mother, who was in the hospital with an advanced state of cancer and, in the middle of the ward, stopped Diana in her tracks. 'Forgive me, but my mother is very ill. It would mean everything to her if you could go and have a few words.'

Without hesitation, Diana walked into her ward and sat with the mother for an hour. The following day, she came again and sat talking to her for a long time. Sadly, the mother died a few weeks later. Princess Diana took it upon herself to telephone the bereaved family, and even invited them to the Palace. They accepted her invitation and spent an hour there talking to Diana. Nobody knew about this, nobody heard about it. Diana's kind gesture meant *everything* to the family. It helped the relatives cope with the mother's passing away. Diana never mentioned this to anyone, but I am mentioning it now and I hope it illustrates her unseen side.

The visits to the hospital were certainly not part of her official schedule. There was no question of publicity. Knowing a little about her, I find some of the accusations about her supposedly using charity to gain publicity and curry favour with the public to be most wicked and evil slanders. I met Diana on a number of occasions. On one particular evening in 1987, we shared a conversation when she attended London's Victoria Palace Theatre for a special charity performance to benefit the Foundation For Children with Leukaemia. Because ours was a fundraising evening, she knew that her attendance would allow us to charge a substantially higher price for the seats. She also brought prestige to the charity.

Afterwards, I spoke to Diana in the green room about the enormous amount of abuse she received from the press and the lampooning on television. I mentioned *Spitting Image* as being particularly cruel and wondered what her and the royal family thought about it. 'Oh, we absolutely love it!' Diana told me. I said, 'But how can you love it? They are really savage to you!' But she insisted, 'No, no, no. We take it in good stead. We think it is very funny, actually. We enjoy the sketches.' I carried on, 'But what about when they are deeply personal about *you*, Diana?' She laughed, 'Well, one learns to accept that one is going to be the victim of lampoons and satires, cartoons and jokes. I laugh at the jokes about other people and I also laugh at the jokes about the royal family.' Diana genuinely surprised me that night and I shall never forget our conversation.

I shared another revealing conversation, this time with Diana's brother-in-law Prince Andrew, when I appeared at a charity golf event at Wentworth about five years ago. The day teed off to a spectacular start when I played my first shot in front of all the TV cameras and press – and my ball bounced on the putting green and shot straight into the pro shop! Everybody thought it was hilarious but I didn't. It was the best shot I played all day.

At the end of the afternoon's sport, we attended a dinner at which Prince Andrew was the guest of honour. I asked him if he would mind if we broke protocol and spoke man to man. He replied that he didn't. I said, 'I realise that you're a sailor and so, would you mind if I use quite salty language?' And Prince Andrew replied, 'No, please go ahead.' So, I said, 'I get it in the neck from the press on a regular basis. But you and Fergie are given a rough deal *all the time* – unremittingly! How do you put up with this nonsense?' They were not precisely, I should add, the exact words I used. The language I *really* used was much fruitier than that! I actually said to him, 'How do you put up with this fucking nonsense in the press?'

Prince Andrew laughed. 'No, no no. One must acknowledge it is very important to have a fair press and they must be allowed freedom of speech,' he said. 'It is one of the great cornerstones of British society and if they decide that they are going to attack, then they must have the freedom to do so.' I said, 'Come off it! This isn't what free speech is meant to be all about. They vilify you! Don't give me the correct, polite answer. Give me the real answer. How do you *really* feel?' And then Andrew started freeing up and went into great detail about the brutality of the press. He talked about how he felt the press had targeted him and his family on a personal level.

It was very obvious that the royals *do* feel bruised and wounded and that they hate the misrepresentation and the lies written about them in the press. Suddenly, in conversation, Andrew became very human and vulnerable. And I learned a valuable lesson that day. No matter how hard and resilient people may appear in public, when they read half-truths about themselves, nonsense and bitter personal attacks, it *does* wound. And that applies just as much to me as it does to any member of the royal family. People like Fergie, Diana and Charles did, and still do, contribute tremendous amounts of very valuable work that is often overlooked.

I was lucky enough to meet Prince Charles when I was invited to a charity polo match at the exclusive Guards Club. Quite a few celebrities attended, including Bruce Forsyth, Susan George and Robert Powell. I spent a long time talking to Dale Tryon, the Australian lady who was once romantically linked to Charles. She and her two lovely daughters, then aged about eight and ten, proved great fun and we sat at the lunch table chatting away. Just before Prince Charles arrived, I was asked to join the normal royal line-up. He came wandering in after his round of golf, sporting a very natty pair of jodhpurs and a Prince of Wales check shirt. I whispered to Dale's girls, 'When the Prince comes round this way, I want you to ask him for his ticket. Say, "I'm sorry, you're not allowed in here without a ticket," or "Please can I see your ticket?"' I thought it would be fun and I have always believed that Charles has quite a ripe sense of humour. As Charles came down the line, meeting the various celebrities, he approached me with a smile. 'Ah yes, I love your programmes,' he said, which was kind. 'Thank you very much,' I said, 'and these two young ladies have a question for you . . .'

The little girls looked up and said, 'You're not allowed in here without a ticket. Can we see your ticket, please?' Charles immediately started smiling, but his equerry, watching like a hawk, quickly pushed him along. His equerry was *deeply unamused* by this bit of harmless chit-chat. In a flash, Prince Charles was gone and I was left thinking, 'That was *so* unkind!' I couldn't have cared less whether it was a bad joke or not. In fact, it was no more than a harmless piece of fun and what upset me was that the children lost out. But the equerry had decided to physically move Charles on. That told me a great deal. In my view, one of the problems with the royal family and their public image is that they are surrounded by people who are completely out of touch with the real world. I had the distinct impression that Charles would have quite enjoyed lingering for that extra little moment with those two girls. But he wasn't allowed to.

Even more sadly, there is a somewhat more serious down-side to fame and celebrity. At one time or another, most celebrities have experienced the obsessive fan or stalker. It is a most uncomfortable feeling. My experience started in 1984 when an attractive girl, aged about twenty-five, asked me for my autograph outside LWT's London studios during a run of *Game For A Laugh*. I didn't think anything of it at the time, and then the next night, I noticed her in the audience again. She caught my eye and I briefly acknowledged her. And then she seemed to be everywhere I went. After each show, she'd wait outside the studio and ask me for my autograph yet again. She'd say, 'How's it going?' and I'd be very friendly back. I found that I couldn't avoid her. She was turning up at the dressing-room door, or waiting outside the studio. And then she somehow managed to find out my home address. To this day, I don't know where she obtained that information. She also seemed to know where I'd be making any personal appearances.

She wrote me a series of letters saying that she wanted to talk to me. She said she had a daughter, although I don't think she'd been married. She kept on, so eventually, after three months, in all innocence, I agreed to meet her. It was probably the worst thing I could have done because, after that, she became relentlessly clingy. I deliberately tried to avoid her. But then she wrote me a further series of letters, this time demanding to know why I was avoiding her. They became more and more obsessive, saying things like, 'How could you be so cruel and heartless?' She said she only wanted us to be close.

One day the vitriol set in. She became increasingly bitter and more threatening, and then somehow managed to discover my home telephone number. Like most celebrities, I am always very careful about giving out my home number, so that was rather disturbing. She started leaving me a series of bizarre messages at all times of the day and night, which culminated in, 'You have betrayed me!' and 'You won't be able to walk down a dark alley without looking behind you, because some day I'll be there!' She was now ringing every day and, although the phone calls were not that long in duration, over a period of about three months, I had maybe one hundred phone calls. Her letters became extremely abusive and more bizarre. Her reign of obsession lasted for about one year. She was writing to me as if we had had some deep emotional and sexual relationship, which I had broken off. The problem was that the more I ignored her, the more she seemed to feel spurned. I just felt sorry for her in the end.

It was very difficult to know how to handle all this. Obviously, I realised I was dealing with somebody who was psychologically disturbed and dependent on attention. In her own mind, she had created a relationship that didn't exist. I saw it as a genuine threat and felt very concerned. I was becoming increasingly worried about how to handle it but, eventually, it all just died away.

Out of interest I have kept all her letters, which carried on arriving at my home for about a year afterwards. I have dozens of them, all very neatly typed, probably twenty letters in all. Then, out of the blue one day about two years ago, I received through the mail, a strange postcard signed by this woman. It appeared she lived in South London and she said how amused she had been to read about the stalking controversy. She added, in a rather chilling tone, that she just wanted me to know that she was still around.

(Sigh) . . . What it is to be famous!

12

WATCH OUT! . . . THIS IS ME

Because I began life where and how I did, I can now recognise my good fortune. I have become a wildly optimistic person. I like to see the good in people and I am a natural enthusiast. Many people confuse my passion for things for plain aggression, and in a sense, I am aggressive. But it is my motor, my passport to achievement. When everybody says, 'No, Jeremy, it can't be done!' that's like a red rag to the bull in Beadle!

I never feel depressed or despondent when obstacles are put in my way. When frustration looms, it only makes me more determined. The way I see things, if I am determined and I enjoy what I am doing, then I don't feel tired, but positive that the efforts I've invested will pay dividends eventually. I feel sure I will reap the rewards.

I've probably been graced with forty or fifty lucky breaks in my life. And all those lucky breaks have been about meeting people. They've been people who have changed me, altered me, inspired me, comforted me, given me love. Part of my philosophy in life is to 'pass on' and I have always tried to pass on whatever I can to others. I think 'passing on' is something we should all do. For example, I always give hitch-hikers a lift. I know what it's like to shiver in the rain in a lay-by, and I still remember what it's like to have no money at all. I know what it's like when a total stranger comes up to you out of the blue and gives you money. It's very obvious that you're hungry and that you have nothing. I have been there. I have passed on that stranger's kindness.

Today I enjoy life. But I still keep in the back of my mind all the time that I am living in an *assumed* state of luxury, comfort and security. Because of my background, I believe that the bubble can burst at any moment. Life can't be *this* good for ever, I reason with myself.

I started out as a naughty, cheeky, mischievous rebel and a seriously bad boy. And now, just because I have turned fifty, I haven't developed into an angel. Far from it! I am cheekier than ever. I am naughtier than ever before. It sounds absurd but I say again that I put much of my success simply down to meeting the right people and to drinking in the right bars.

If you pick the right people to travel with through life, as I have done . . . then you'd better Watch Out! Who knows, soon, the star of the show could be you!

PICTURE CREDITS

The plates in this book emanate from the following sources, to whom the publishers gratefully offer acknowledgement. The authors and publishers have made all reasonable efforts to contact copyright holders for permission, and any omissions or errors in the form of credit given will be corrected in future editions.